Carolina Lily

New Quilts from an Old Favorite

edited by Linda Baxter Lasco

American Quilter's Society

P.O. Box 3290 • Paducah, KY 42002-3290
Fax 270-898-1173 • e-mail: orders@AQSquilt.com

Thank You, Sponsors

JANOME

Located in Paducah, Kentucky, the American Quilter's Society (AQS) is dedicated to promoting the accomplishments of today's quilters. Through its publications and events, AQS strives to honor today's quiltmakers and their work and to inspire future creativity and innovation in quiltmaking.

Executive Book Editor: Elaine H. Brelsford
Senior Book Editor: Linda Baxter Lasco
Copy Editor: Chrystal Abhalter
Proofreader: Joann Treece
Graphic Design: Lynda Smith
Cover Design: Michael Buckingham
Quilt Photography: Charles R. Lynch

Additional copies of this book may be ordered from the American Quilter's Society, PO Box 3290, Paducah, KY 42002-3290, or online at www.AmericanQuilter.com.

Text © 2014, American Quilter's Society
Artwork © 2014, American Quilter's Society

American Quilter's Society
P.O. Box 3290 • Paducah, KY 42002-3290
Fax 270-898-1173 • e-mail: orders@AQSquilt.com

Library of Congress Cataloging-in-Publication Data

Carolina Lily : new quilts from an old favorite / edited by Linda Baxter Lasco.
    pages cm
  Includes bibliographical references and index.
  ISBN 978-1-60460-137-4 (alk. paper)
  1. Quilts--United States--Pictorial works. 2. Flowers in art-
-Pictorial works. 3. Quilting--Competitions--United States. I.
Lasco, Linda Baxter.
II. National Quilt Museum.
  NK9112.C37 2014
  746.46074--dc23
                                    2014008455

Cover: ONLY A LILY, detail. Full quilt on page 11.
Title Page: RADIANT BLOOMS. Full quilt on page 37.

Dedication

This book is dedicated to all those who see a traditional quilt and visualize both its link to the past and its bridge to the future.

"Honoring Today's Quilter"

THE NATIONAL QUILT MUSEUM

The National Quilt Museum (NQM) is an exciting place where the public can learn more about quilts, quiltmaking, quiltmakers, and experience quilts that inspire and delight.

The museum celebrates today's quilts and quiltmakers through exhibits of quilts from the museum's collection and selected temporary exhibits. By providing a variety of workshops and other programs, The National Quilt Museum helps to encourage, inspire, and enhance the development of today's quilter.

Whether presenting new or antique quilts, the museum promotes understanding of and respect for all quilts—contemporary and antique, classical and innovative, machine made and handmade, utility and art.

Contents

Preface

While preservation of the past is one of The National Quilt Museum's core functions, one of its greatest services is performed as it links the past to the present and to the future. With that goal in mind, The National Quilt Museum sponsors an annual contest and exhibit—New Quilts from an Old Favorite (NQOF).

Created both to acknowledge our quiltmaking heritage and to recognize innovation, creativity, and excellence, the contest challenges today's quiltmakers to interpret a single traditional quilt block in a new and exciting work of their own design. Each year, contestants respond with a myriad of stunning interpretations.

Carolina Lily: New Quilts from an Old Favorite is a collection of these interpretations. In this book, you'll find a brief description of the 2014 contest, followed by the five award winners and 13 additional finalists and their quilts.

Full-color photographs of the quilts accompany each quiltmaker's comments—comments that provide insight into their widely diverse creative processes. Patterns for traditional Carolina Lily blocks are included to give you a starting point for your own rendition. The winners' and finalists' tips and techniques offer an artistic framework for your own interpretation. In addition, some information about The National Quilt Museum is included.

Our wish is that *Carolina Lily: New Quilts from an Old Favorite* will further our quiltmaking heritage as new quilts based on these blocks are inspired by the outstanding quilts contained within.

Left: REBORN, detail. Full quilt on page 71.

The Contest

Quilts must be recognizable in some way as a variation on that year's selected block. The quilts must be no larger than 80" and no smaller than 50" on a side. Each quilt entered must be quilted. Quilts may only be entered by the maker(s) and must have been completed after December 31 two years prior to the entry date.

Quiltmakers are asked to send in two images—one of the full quilt and one detail—for jurying. Three jurors view these and consider technique, artistry, and interpretation of the theme block to select 18 finalists. These finalist quilts are sent to the museum where a panel of three judges carefully evaluates them. This evaluation of the actual quilts focuses on design, innovation, theme, and workmanship. The first-through fifth-place winners are then selected and notified.

An exhibit of the 18 quilts opens at The National Quilt Museum in Paducah, Kentucky, each spring and then travels to venues around the country for two years. Thousands of quilt lovers have enjoyed these exhibits at their local or regional museum.

A book is published by the American Quilter's Society featuring full-color photos of all the finalists and quilts, biographical information about each quilter, and their tips and techniques. The book provides an inside look at how quilts are created and a glimpse into the artistic mindset of today's quilters.

Previous theme blocks have been Double Wedding Ring, Log Cabin, Kaleidoscope, Mariner's Compass, Ohio Star, Pineapple, Storm at Sea, Bear's Paw, Tumbling Blocks, Feathered Star, Monkey Wrench, Seven Sisters, Dresden Plate, Sawtooth, Sunflower, Orange Peel, Baskets, and Jacob's Ladder. The block selected for 2014 was Carolina Lily. The 2015 block will be Nine Patch. New York Beauty and Flying Geese will be the featured blocks for 2016 and 2017, respectively.

NQM would like to thank this year's New Quilts from an Old Favorite contest sponsors: Janome and Moda Fabrics.

Left: CAROLINA IN MY MIND, detail. Full quilt on page 57.

The Carolina Lily Block

The Carolina Lily block reflects the desire for beauty using the language of flowers. It is closely related to Tulip, Peony, Poinsettia, and Carnation blocks in structure. Many quilts made of these patterns look so similar that it is no wonder they are often confused. In Barbara Brackman's *Encyclopedia of Pieced Quilt Patterns*, there are just two patterns named Carolina Lily, but there are 28 patterns that are extremely similar. These include Meadow Lily, Wood Lily, Prairie Lily, Fire Lily, Basket of Lilies, Tulip in Vase, and Basket of Tulips. A few such published patterns may be from as early as 1889, but the most are from the 1930s. Brackman's #743 Carolina Lily was also published on February 15, 1890, as Royal Japanese Vase in *Farm and Home*; #768.2 was published in *Ohio Farmer* in 1896 with the name Tree Quilt Pattern.[1]

Fifty-one CAROLINA LILY quilts found on the Quilt Index website suggest that the Carolina Lily block was popular from the mid-1800s on. This coincides with the pronounced increase in the number of periodicals due to technological advances in linotype after the Civil War. This resulted in quilt patterns being published and syndicated, available to practically every quilter in America. It also follows the rise of block-style quilts as the predominant form in the mid-1800s.

Laurel Horton notes that during the Civil War, "...the major portion of downtown Columbia [South Carolina] and its homes were destroyed in a fire during the city's occupation by Sherman's troops. Very few antebellum quilts from Columbia survived compared with other parts of the state."[2] In addition, "...by the second year of the war most South Carolinians felt the effect of shortages resulting from the blockade imposed on southern ports....[the result was that]...calicoes were imported, primarily from Europe...[the use of sewing machines] was hampered by lack of proper thread. Handspun thread was unsuitable and imported."[3] Such privations didn't stop women from making quilts, and it is likely that any quilts made during this period were treasured.

Quilters have always loved fabric. In her study of Macon County, North Carolina, quilts, Horton found that "... as elsewhere during the early nineteenth century, blankets were cheap and available and quilts were special creations. A woman planning to spend the time and effort to make a quilt was likely also to have gone to the expense to purchase fabric especially for that quilt."[4] Fabrics were available in the 1870s and 1880s in the Piedmont due to rapid development of the local textile industry. The port of Charleston also imported more elegant fabrics from Europe.[5]

We must pay homage to our quilting forebearers. What would we do if we couldn't have any fabric we wanted? What if we couldn't even find thread? Those women made lovely quilts in spite of what was swirling in the world around them. The Carolina Lily block is testament to that.

Judy Schwender
Curator, The National Quilt Museum

[1] Barbara Brackman, *Encyclopedia of Pieced Quilt Designs*, American Quilter's Society, 1993.

[2] Laurel Horton, "South Carolina's Traditional Quilts" in *Uncoverings*, 1984, Volume 5 of the Research Papers of the American Quilt Study Group, Sally Garoutte, editor; AQSG, 1984, 64.

[3] Laurel Horton, "South Carolina Quilts and the Civil War" in *Uncoverings*, 1985, Volume 6 of the Research Papers of the American Quilt Study Group, Sally Garoutte, editor; AQSG, 1985, 59-60.

[4] Laurel Horton, "Nineteenth Century Middle Class Quilts in Macon County, North Carolina" in *Uncoverings*, 1983, Volume 4 of the Research Papers of the American Quilt Study Group, Sally Garoutte, editor; AQSG, 1983, 93.

[5] Horton, "South Carolina's Traditional Quilts," 63.

THE NATIONAL QUILT MUSEUM

First Place
Julia Graber

Brooksville, Mississippi

Photo by Amy J. Graber

Meet Julia

I grew up along the banks of North River in Bridgewater, Virginia, in a family of seven girls and one boy. After graduating from high school I attended Rosedale Bible Institute, served one year of voluntary service with Northern Light Gospel Missions in Ontario, Canada, came to Mississippi where I taught school for three years, and married Paul Graber in 1977. We live on a farm raising hogs and growing corn, soybeans, wheat, and cotton. Paul also helps his brother run a trucking company hauling stone, wood chips, grain, and fertilizer. We have six children and enjoy eight (and counting!) grandchildren.

My interest in sewing started when I was young and I learned to make my own clothes. I made a few tied comforters in my late teens, and after I married, I continued making a few utility quilts for family, friends, charity, and myself. It was after our youngest child started school that the quilting bug really bit me. My sister Polly coaxed me to subscribe to *Quilters Newsletter* magazine which opened my eyes to the quilting world out there. My local guild, the Possum Town Quilters, and the Mississippi Quilting Association have also provided me with encouragement and inspiration.

It wasn't until the late 1990s that I learned to enjoy and appreciate art quilts. I like a new twist or contemporary flavor to the old and traditional and The National Quilt Museum's NQOF contest each year provides just that.

In the year 2000, P&B Textiles donated fabric to guilds that would make charity quilts for the Kosovo refugees. I was president of our Magnolia Sewing Circle at the time and I soon had 100 yards of fabric at my doorstep. Here we are with 10 of the 14 quilts we made for this project.

In recent years, four generations of the women in our family get together for a week to ten days to sew and quilt. We talk, laugh, stay up late, and take turns fixing meals. These times together are one of the highlights of the year for me.

Inspiration, Design & Technique

When my sister Emily started making quilts using Gloria Loughman's technique from her book *Radiant Landscapes: Transform Tiled Colors & Textures into Dramatic Quilts* (C&T Publishing, 2013), I loved the effect. I bought the book, too,

ONLY A LILY

56½" x 56½"

studied it, and decided to make a lily quilt to practice for my entry. I used a commercial dyed cotton for my background, cut out squares of the same fabric, and fused them to the background.

Then I cut out the motifs of the Carolina Lily from black fabric and placed them on top of the background and added a border of black with more Carolina Lily motifs.

I was pleased with how LILY turned out and decided to use the technique for my entry. So, I found a piece of fabric that I thought would work for the background.

I cut red and green squares of two other pieces of fabric, traced a portion of the motif of the traditional Carolina Lily pattern onto the squares, and cut them out.

When Emily saw my little bits of scraps left over she decided to make a small art quilt using them in the sky of her SETTING SAGE quilt.

I thought it marvelous and decided to change my background to the same yellow that she had chosen. But alas, it didn't have the same effect that her's did. So I went back to my original choice of background fabric and I loved what I saw. Here, I have added a black border with slight curves.

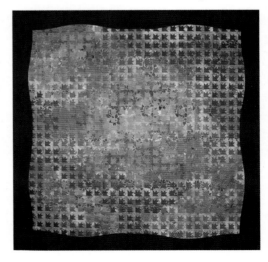

Then I cut out lily parts and laid them on the background. Deciding which lily I liked best was a hard choice.

When all the fusing was finished I was ready to quilt.

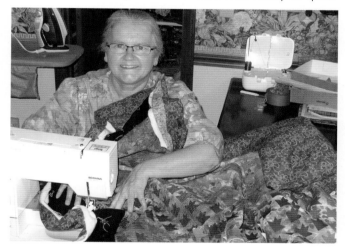

Afterward, the finished quilt wanted to wobble, ripple, and pucker up. But that didn't cause me too much worry as it all flattened out when I blocked it with lots of water. I added the piping and binding and blocked it again.

"I am only . . . a [humble] lily of the valley [that grows in deep and difficult places]. Like the lily among thorns, so are you . . ." (Song of Solomon 2:1, 2 Amplified).

You may visit my blog at http://juliagraber. blogspot.com or e-mail me at pjgraber@juno.com.

Second Place
Karen Watts

Mayhill, New Mexico

Photo by Don Watts

Meet Karen

Quilting has given me so much pleasure over the years that it's hard to imagine what I would have been doing if I had not been a quilter. Perhaps I would have cooked more, done more laundry, or cleaned more often? Not likely, so I guess it's a good thing I have some quilts to show for all that time not spent doing chores!

Of course, when my two children were young, I didn't get to spend as much time quilting as I liked, but I sandwiched it in between Girl Scouts (I was a leader for 12 years), Special Olympics with my son, and volunteering at the elementary school. Now that they are grown, I can spend more time going to retreats, quilt shows, and, of course, quilting at home. But housework? Not so much.

One unexpected pleasure is the friends I have made through quilting. And it's not just local friends met through my guild or in my neighborhood, but nationwide friends I have gotten to know from going to national shows, entering contests, and the Internet community (specifically, www.thequiltshow.com).

The New Quilts from an Old Favorite contest has been so much fun for a couple reasons: first, because I love doing challenges and it's cool to have your quilt in a book and touring the country; second, because it was through the contest that I met Robin Gausebeck, who has become a very

dear friend. Robin entered the contest for the first time the same year as I (Sawtooth, 2008) and we met at the book signing the following year. Now we get together every year for the Paducah show. We went to a Ricky Tims retreat together and also got to spend some time together at the IQA Houston show in November 2013. If not for this contest, I would probably not know Robin.

This is my seventh year to enter the NQOF contest. I think I'll keep entering as long as I have ideas. I know some people say that an artist should develop a style that is their own, but I don't think I have done that. I don't work in a series. I try to do something new and different with every original quilt I design. I don't think people could look at my body of work and know it was all made by the same person. Is this a bad thing? I don't know, but I do have a lot of fun.

Inspiration & Design

The design of LILY PATCH really began with a small bundle of dupioni silk purchased at the International Quilt Festival one year. The bundle was a rainbow of rich, saturated colors and I wanted to use them! Using silk in my quilt made me think of crazy quilts, and the idea came to have more traditional pieced lilies surrounding more freeform appliquéd lilies on a crazy-patch background. I needed to have some sort of division between the areas, so curvy flying geese seemed to work well.

LILY PATCH

54" x 54"

I drew my own lily pattern using Electric Quilt® (EQ7) software, trying several designs until I was satisfied. Here are three of the blocks I drew; the third one is the one I used in the quilt.

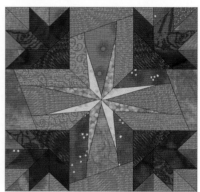

I filled the center area with curvy, flowing leaves and lilies using machine appliqué with a buttonhole stitch. My first thought for the borders was to appliqué more curvy leaves on them. I wanted to see how that would look before I fused them and (maybe) ruined my borders, so I made mock-ups in Adobe® Photoshop® software. I had one border pieced, so I took a photo of the center and one border and made these mock-ups to help me decide what would be best.

As for color, I had many different blue and purple silks, and the background color that really made them pop was RED! I loved the contrast between the rich purples, the red, and the green leaves. In keeping with the crazy-quilt idea, I embroidered small designs in the green area of the flowers.

I started piecing the Lily blocks before I really knew what would be in the center of the quilt, but knew I wanted crazy-patch borders. The initial EQ7 drawing looked like this:

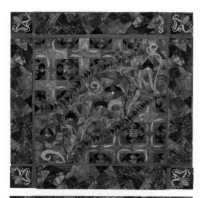

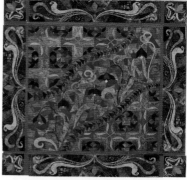

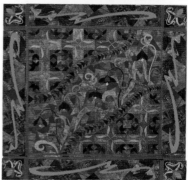

I'm glad I went through that exercise because I found the green in the borders was too distracting. I ended up just quilting lots of different designs in the borders—a new definition of "crazy quilting."

Technique

I used many techniques in this quilt including paper piecing, machine appliqué, and hand embroidery. There are two elements that I had not done before—working with silks and making the curvy flying geese.

Dupioni silk is beautiful, but you need to add a step before you try to piece with it. It will fray badly no matter how careful you are, even after it's pieced, so it's best to use an iron-on interfacing before cutting out your pieces. I used a tricot fusible interfacing, which preserves the soft hand of the silk and prevents fraying. It is the same product used by many quilters to back T-shirts when making T-shirt quilts. Use a low setting on your iron, fuse the tricot, then cut.

The curvy flying geese were fun and easy, although I did spend some time trying to decide how to attach the units to my quilt top. But first, I had to draw them. EQ7 makes this easy with the swath tool. Using your mouse, you can draw a spine for the geese, then edit it for precision. There are tools to change the contour (all one width, wide to narrow, wide in the middle, etc.), the style (triangles or diamonds), width, and boldness. Once you have your swath exactly how you like it, you click "convert to patch" and you're done. The design can be printed as a block, templates, or as a foundation pattern.

Here are some examples of how your flying geese can look.

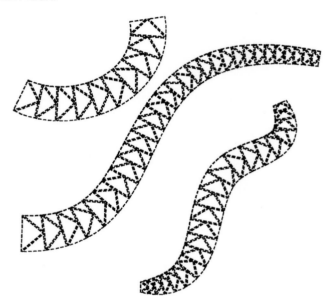

I chose to paper piece mine. As for adding them to my quilt top, I could see two options—piecing or appliqué. Piecing the geese to the rest of the completed blocks would have required me to cut the quilt top very precisely in four places (one cut for each side of the two units), and that just sounded too scary.

I opted for appliqué. I placed the geese where I wanted them and pinned extensively. Being curvy, they could move around a lot. I prepared a very narrow folded bias strip exactly like you would make for binding, lined up the raw edges of the bias strip and the geese units, and stitched on my machine with a straight stitch. Then I folded the bias strip over and handstitched it in place. Once the geese were all stitched down, I cut away the top behind the units to reduce bulk.

Third Place
Mami Noda
Yokkaichi, Mie, Japan

Photo by Mayuka Noda

Meet Mami

The first time I made a quilt was when I became pregnant with my first child. I wanted to wrap the baby warmly with a hand-made quilt. So my quiltmaking life started. Day by day, I have been making quilts. As I do, more and more I notice the depth of the quilt world. I have been increasingly attracted by its charm.

Of course, I have a busy life like every other woman. I pick up scraps of time that are scattered around my daily life—for example, a few minutes waiting until the water boils, or time waiting for a child to come home. We have a lot of such little pieces of time. Don't you think that there is considerably more time if I collect them?

I think it's important that a woman expresses herself. In my case, it is by making quilts. I am happier to have a needle in my hand than at any other time.

Someone may look at my quilt 100 years from now and wonder what kind of person it was who made it. By then, I won't be here anymore, but I am glad there will be someone imagining me. So I think I have to do my best for my quilts.

I think that I can make a good quilt even if I do not use any special materials. It is possible to make an extraordinary quilt with popular fabrics, easily available everywhere. Color combination, design, and technique can make the quilt splendid. Of course, I would also like to use special Japanese fabrics in my quilts.

Inspiration

There is a variety of stimuli in the world. I am inspired by everything to see, to hear, and to feel around me in my life. Sometimes I feel that an angel comes down to me. She whispers a little hint that leads me to make a quilt. Thanks!

Technique

Before I made AUTUMN LILY, I had made a mini-quilt of the same pattern. It was done with a lovely Japanese taupe color. I decided I would like to make it as a big quilt. It is simple and modest, yet still attractive.

AUTUMN LILY

67" x 67"

with lots of love.

Mami Noda — *Autumn Lily*

I planned the placement of the lilies, then added a Log Cabin border to add movement.

I added trapunto to add a three-dimensional effect. I will leave it up to the observer as to whether or not the design succeeded.

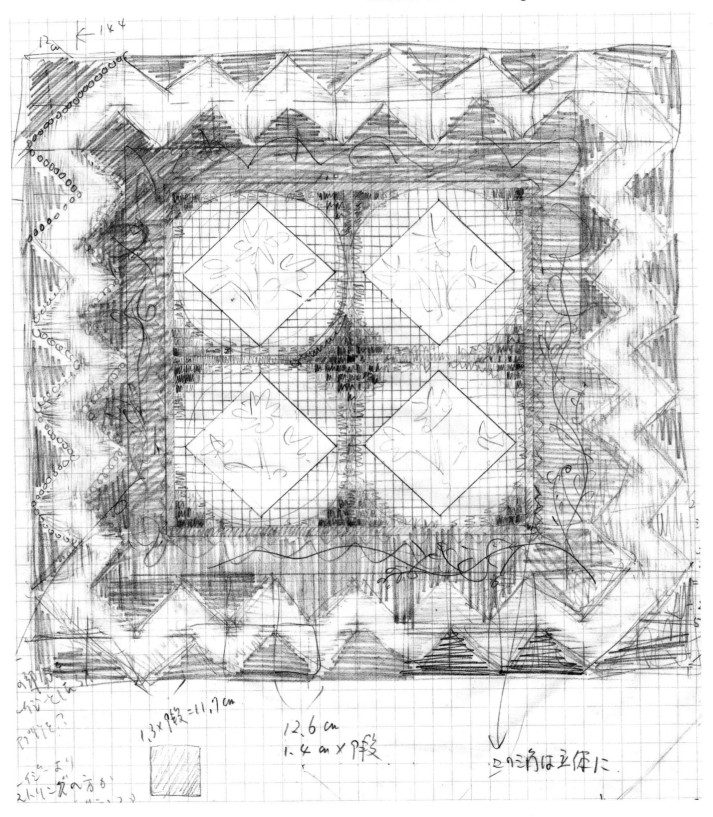

Fourth Place

Marilyn Smith
Columbia, Missouri

Photo by Cheryl Morris

Photo by Marilyn Smith

Rachel Weekley
Montgomery City, Missouri

Rachel's Story

I have been sewing since I was eight and in 4-H. My mom, Marilyn Smith, was my sewing leader and I had a lot of practice at home! I have sewn many garments and projects over the years and continue to do so. I grew up watching my grandmother and her friends sitting around the quilting frame. Though I helped at times, I never felt a connection to quilting. It wasn't until my mother began quilting and had her first quilt in the quilt show in Paducah that I began to see the diversity of quilting and take interest in the art. I went to Paducah that year and when I saw how vast the designs and techniques were, I decided that I wanted to learn more. I made my first quilt before I had my son, Garrett, now six, and then another for my daughter, Jillian, now five.

Of course, with two small children, time was and is still limited. I started by doing something new with my daughter's quilt—learning how to free-motion quilt—and I fell in love. I have since started my own creation, but finding the time to work on and finish it is hard! I am learning to use my afternoons while my daughter is at preschool. I enjoy everything from sewing and crafting to quilting. I love collaborating with my mom. She has so much to teach me and we work well together.

I have been a certified Zumba® instructor since 2010 and I volunteer my time teaching classes at churches. I love to do this. It allows me to stay fit and I also get to help others in their journey to better health! I am involved in our church where I lead Zumba, teach nursery once a month, help with special events and Vacation Bible School, and participate in women's Bible studies. I have been married for nine years to my husband, Matt. We own a farm close to our home and love to spend time there—riding four wheelers, exploring the woods, helping during planting and harvest, giving rides to and from the fields, and feeding the guys.

Marilyn's Story

I have been building my dream home since the end of June and have been so busy with that, family, and church activities that I hadn't sat at my sewing machine very much during the summer. I was really itching to get back to creating something for the New Quilts from an Old Favorite contest, but I had done very little. I had purchased fabric at Hancock's of Paducah that I planned to cut it up for *broderie perse,* a technique that I had never used but wanted to learn.

With the deadline just one month away, I asked my daughter, Rachel, if she would like to collaborate on a quilt. I was surprised and excited when she said, "Yes." I sent her home with some of the fabric to cut out for *broderie perse.* We planned our next meeting at her house (an hour away from mine) to talk about design.

I love the NQOF contest and have previously entered quilts for the Burgoyne Surrounded, Baskets, and Jacob's Ladder contests. My quilt SYCAMORE BARK BASKETS was accepted into the

JILLI'S LILIES

52" x 68"

exhibit in 2012. One of the things I like about this contest is the challenge—and the quick turnaround. You can post the quilt to the quilt museum one day, hear the jurors' decision two weeks later, and hear the judges' decisions two weeks after that.

I really like entering quilts in quilt shows. My quilts have hung in Paducah, Houston, Grand Rapids, Lancaster, Road to California, Phoenix, Nashville, and Des Moines. It is always a thrill to be accepted. Winning an award is just icing on the cake. As a mom, this collaboration with Rachel is very special and precious to me.

Marilyn—Inspiration & Design

We began at the end of September with what I had envisioned for the design of this quilt. My vision was four large equal-sized Lily blocks placed symmetrically on the background with *broderie perse* flowers on top of the Lily blocks. We tried different placements but nothing seemed to make our hearts sing. We decided to lay the flowers aside and concentrate on the placement of the Lily blocks on the background. We had to think more "outside the box."

Knowing that asymmetrical designs look best with an uneven number of parts, we discarded one of the blocks and began to try various placements on the background. Rachel's son decided to "help" and much to our astonishment, his placement of the blocks to the outside of the edges of the background looked much better.

We realized that the blocks needed to be bigger to meet the size requirement and decided that making three different size blocks would be more appealing. Using freezer paper, we made templates for the three blocks.

The next design decision was color. We threw caution to the wind and decided that we should use bold, bright solids for this quilt. I volunteered to go shopping for fabric. My daughter's last words to me were, "Don't make it look too Halloween by using orange, purple, and black."

Rachel—Color & Placement

When I saw the fabric Mom had purchased, I was slightly stunned. Halloween colors were exactly what I was looking at! I decided to make the flower petals orange and the rest of the block purple, with a black background for the maximum effect. I put Wonder-Under® fusible web on the back of the fabric and cut out the pieces from the templates we had designed. I then ironed them in place on the background, making sure that all the edges were straight and that the pieces of the block were separated from each other evenly, giving the blocks an exploded effect.

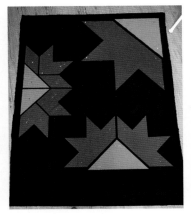

When it was all ironed down, I knew that our Halloween colors were perfect. I returned the quilt to Mom so that she could put the satin stitching around each piece.

Marilyn—Raw-Edge Appliqué

I used raw-edge appliqué to set the pieces permanently on the background. I used narrow satin stitching with thread matching each fabric. Then I did linear spiral quilting on the two smaller Lily blocks. I quilted them with the feed dogs up and used the edge of my ¼" presser foot as a guide. I soon realized I would have trouble with puckering so I decided to quilt a free-motion freeform feather pattern and had good results with it.

Rachel and I talked about how we would do the background quilting and decided to make it a whimsical garden of flowers. We both love to free-motion quilt using our home sewing machines and I have to admit that she is better at it than I. We had chosen a variegated thread and would use it as well as the corresponding solid colors in the thread to quilt the background.

I had some whimsical flower templates that I had made for another quilt and began quilting them across the quilt, first marking them with a fine white pencil. Meanwhile, Rachel began making original whimsical flower templates of her own designs.

Rachel—Flowers

I was able to find time to work on this quilt because Mom would watch and play with my kids while I worked for hours at the sewing machine. Since quilting is a very creative outlet for me, I find it relaxing and enjoy the time that I spend doing it! We passed the quilt back and forth between ourselves every few days and worked to combine our quilting techniques across the quilt evenly.

I drew my own templates of the flowers I wanted to quilt. My first and favorite flower is heart shapes put together; see if you can find it!

When it was my turn to quilt, I marked the outline of my flowers with a thin white pencil and then let my creative juices flow to design the insides with free-motion quilting. I had suggested to Mom that we make the quilt look as if it were framed like a piece of art, leaving the bottom of the quilt almost blank, but when we got to that point, we decided to add more visual interest and create the line of flowers growing from the bottom; the vertical lines help to draw the eye to the main part of the quilt. I think the effect is very dramatic and appealing.

Marilyn—Background Quilting

Now it was time to do the background quilting. Rachel knew she wanted it done with an organic leaf and vine quilting design to correspond to the garden theme. We talked at length and decided that the pattern would be more consistent in design if done by one person. She free-motion quilted and I played with the kids. (We both think we got the better deal!) She did a wonderful job. I took the quilt home to bind, make a hanging sleeve, and block it, while Rachel made the label. It was finally finished—all except the name.

We call Rachel's daughter Jilli. She has such a sweet personality and was always interested in what her mother was doing at the sewing machine. We decided to name our quilt after her: JILLI'S LILIES. Rachel will tell you that she likes the name because Jillian has a lot of personality and is full of energy, just like the flowers we quilted!

We ran the lint brush over it, boxed it up, and mailed it to Paducah, two days before the deadline. We had done it!!!

Fifth Place
Jean B. Freestone
Osprey, Florida

Photo by Frank J. Freestone

Meet Jean

I first discovered quilting in 1999 when I retired from teaching kindergarten and first grade in New Jersey. I was feeling at a loss, not able to define who I was since I was no longer "teacher" and my mother role was diminished with both daughters in college. I happened on a quilting book in the public library and was instantly hooked. I went to a local quilt show, joined a quilt guild, read every book in the guild library, and was thankfully taken under the wing by some very knowledgeable ladies who loved hand appliqué, like me! I was on my way!

I enjoy technique classes but am happier digging into quilt books and magazines for possible new ideas. This allows reflection and sketching time! My father, an architect, and my mother, a home economics teacher, encouraged me in all my creative endeavors. I inherited my love of design and sewing from them. I enjoy collecting and using Japanese fabrics and have done many quilts with an oriental theme. Since moving to Florida and living on a beautiful pond, I find the theme of water becoming more prevalent in my work. With my husband of 45 years being an avid kayaker, I am never lacking for water inspiration. He was very happy when I recently made a kayaking quilt for him. Quilting has opened doors for me with new friendships, fantastic cottage groups, plus the wider community of two quilt guilds in Venice and Sarasota.

I have never made a traditional quilt but the tradition of quilting and what has come before is important to me. Each quilt I make has some new technique I want to try, so I am forever learning. The "something new" that I tried in this quilt was painting on silk. Hand appliqué, research, creative design, and paying attention to detail have all been the most enjoyable aspects of quilting for me.

With my machine quilting slowly improving, what was a challenge is now another pleasurable aspect of quilting. I have learned to love the whole process. I have a stash but refuse to grow out of the one closet I designate for its use. I know the challenge of moving to smaller quarters and getting rid of things! Therefore, this quilt was made entirely from my stash except for the backing. My goal is to make a few good quilts in my lifetime, so I spend lots of time on each quilt. I have been blessed with quite a few ribbons, so I am happy that my quilts speak to other people, too.

Inspiration & Design

Because I enjoy seeing how other quilters approach creative design, the books published about the New Quilts from an Old Favorite contest have been a must for me to collect. This quilt has definitely been a challenge but I'm glad I pushed through to finish and enter.

I have always wanted to try my hand at the creative challenge of designing a quilt for The National Quilt Museum competition. I saw that the 2014 block was the Carolina Lily and, by adding one word, it became a must for me to

CAROLINA WATER LILY

60" x 61"

enter! Making my CAROLINA WATER LILY quilt had my mind swimming with ideas!

I searched the Web to find a Carolina Lily block that showed a possibility of a lily pond. Then I started sketching. The finished quilt ended up almost exactly like the original sketch with two fully open lilies and one bud dipping under water.

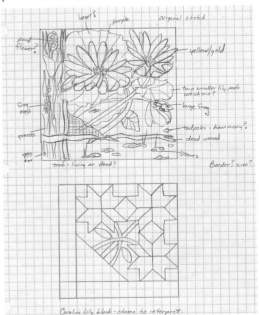

I wanted the waterline toward the top third of the quilt so I kept the block's sashing and cornerstone in the design to push the flowers higher. I defined the inner edges of the sashing with wood—a horizontal decaying log and a vertical young tree. The tree also divided the pond from the shoreline grasses and water hyacinth. Now, what to do with the cornerstone? How do I make it separate but connected to the theme of the quilt? Solution: it became a copy of the Carolina Lily block done in stone fabric and beads. This also tied into the other stones found on the pond bottom.

Other design questions appeared. How do I present the triangle from which the lilies grow? I found in my pond research that you can plant the lily tubers in a container or basket. It is best placed at an angle against the side of the pond to allow air to escape. Also, if the pond freezes solid in the winter, you can remove the lily, container and all, to submerge in the spring. Voilá! The

triangle became an old woven basket, slowly falling apart from being kept submerged, since, in Florida, my pond will never freeze!

The basket was made by pressing wet, wrinkled fabric into a triangular shape. I then fused slivers of brown fabric into the wrinkles to create a very dirty, dilapidated basket. Since two lily leaves are also in the Carolina Lily block, I took artistic license to make one extremely large, behind the lilies, and a small new leaf floating to the surface.

The last design question: Why is the lily bud faced down underwater? The answer hopped onto the drawing in the form of a large frog climbing out of the pond to catch a dragonfly lunch.

Since frogs are a biological early warning indicator of a pond's health (and I wanted a healthy pond), frogs arrived on my quilt in all their stages of metamorphosis: eggs, tadpoles, and adults!

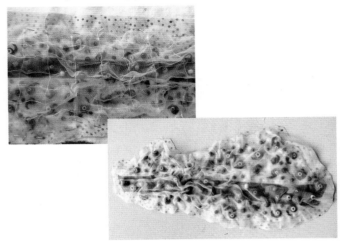

The copyright-free Dover coloring book *NatureScapes* by Patricia J. Wynne helped with the frog design. The gelatinous mass of frog eggs, shown clinging to a blade of grass on the pond's edge, was made with beads under silk organza. Other pond inhabitants slipped onto the quilt by being quilted in the border.

Technique

My most challenging part of the construction process was to paint each individual lily petal. I selected one of my photographs showing two separate water lilies. After deciding on the finished quilt size, I traced and enlarged the open water lilies with an Artograph Tracer® projector. Each petal was individually drawn on the shiny side of freezer paper with all shadow areas indicated.

Silk was ironed on top with markings showing through the silk. Each petal was then painted with Setacolor® Transparent Paint and Lightening Medium. I wanted one purple and one yellow lily. After two attempts, I got the colors I wanted. I found that by adding a little purple to the yellow paint, the two lily colors were compatible.

To stop shadowing, I lined each petal with light fusible woven lining cut exactly to the size of the petal pattern. This duo was then ironed back

onto individual freezer paper patterns and turned under. I now had many different petals to hand appliqué into two lilies.

I often use an appliqué technique that I learned from an *American Quilter* magazine article (Spring 2004) entitled "Hand Appliqué a Different Way" by Frances B. Calhoun. She appliqués first onto tissue paper! I have perfected this technique over the years. The outline of the whole unit is drawn on tissue paper. The individual parts are cut out of freezer paper and ironed to the selected fabrics. The fabric is cut ¼" away from the pattern, and the edges are starched and pressed under. They are all then hand-basted to the tissue paper instead of the fabric background. Hand appliqué is completed on all inner edges.

Using a camera, I can audition unit placement on various fabric backgrounds. After the final decision, I gently pull the unit away from the tissue paper, remove the basting and freezer paper, and then baste only the edges for final appliqué to the chosen background. The two units of water lily stamens were done the same way, and then slid into each lily center for final appliqué.

I find that my way of creating quilts with elements done in paper patterns and unit appliqué is much like making a bulletin board from my teaching days. What a wonderful connection between two parts of my life.

The top is complete! Now quilting designs were sketched and practiced, and thread color was determined—but that is a whole other story!

Janice Averill
West Haven, Connecticut

Photo by Timothy C. Averill

Janice Roy
Bridgeport, Connecticut

Photo by Mark R. Roy

Meet Janice Averill

My fascination with sewing started at an early age. After high school, I earned a degree in fashion design at the Fashion Institute of Technology in New York City. I worked at Warnaco Lingerie for a short spell as a design estimator. While raising my family I pursued a part-time career as a custom clothier. After taking a class in fabric dyeing, I began to see that I could exercise my creative nature through quilting.

The best part about quilting is that there are no fittings involved! Quilts never go out of style and the gift of a quilt is like a hug from the quilter. Quilting also satisfies a Connecticut Yankee instinct—frugality. No matter how spectacular a quilt is, it still has a practical use as a bed covering. As much as I loved designing and making formal wear, it's not practical.

I find inspiration and ideas for designs everywhere I go. I've made friends and family crazy because I keep stopping to study random patterns that I see or compositions that appeal to my eyes. I didn't start off with a natural eye for color and composition. Instead, I developed my design skills over the past decade through a lot of reading and experimentation. My basic philosophy of color theory, as it pertains to quilt design, is that you need to have a variety of textures and values among your fabric choices.

I'm lucky to have a husband and children who wholeheartedly support my creative endeavors. None of this would be possible without their encouragement. I also have to give credit for my journey to my quilt guild, the Connecticut Piecemakers. Being a member has helped me improve as a quilter and a designer. The chance to become a quilt designer came to me through one of their monthly meetings.

Finding time to fit quilting into my life isn't an issue for me, as I'm fortunate enough to have made quilting my career. I design quilting projects for Quilting Treasures fabric collections. I've had the opportunity to design a couple of their Block-of-the Month quilts. Plus my quilts have appeared in publications such as *Fons & Porter's Love of Quilting* and *Quiltmaker* magazines.

I met Janice Roy when she joined our guild. After she quilted some of my quilts, I knew I had met someone I could collaborate with on a project. Working with Janice has been a lot of fun and we're already thinking about next year's NQOF Nine-Patch theme. Plus we're hoping to complete a project for the Hoffman Challenge. After that maybe we'll tackle the International Quilt Festival in Houston. The sky's the limit.

Meet Janice Roy

I am the descendant of a creative family and very early in my life developed a love for needle arts.

ZEN LILIES

50" x 50"

My interest in quilting developed in my 20s. I loved the mix of colors, prints, and the endless number of quilt designs I would see in magazines. I waited to take a beginner quilting class until my two boys were old enough to be more independent. Once I started, I WAS HOOKED!

In 2002, as both my husband and I faced losing our corporate jobs, we decided to open a quilting business. We ran a large quilting studio until 2009. I still have one of those machines, named Yang. It has become my best friend ever since. I learn something new with Yang every day.

The versatility of a system that can be either computer- or hand-driven affords me endless finishing flexibility. My husband is very talented at digitizing designs and so we work together to create patterns for the quilts that I work on. One of our first customers was Denyse Schmidt of Denyse Schmidt Quilts. It has been my pleasure to provide my machine quilting and binding services to Denyse for more than 10 years. Many of her quilts have been featured in magazines and shown as an art collection in many museums, including The National Quilt Museum!

I especially enjoy the opportunity to quilt pieces for others. I see many different quilts made with many different techniques and get to fondle fabric every day. My life is filled with color, design and the beaming faces of my clients when they see their quilt finished. What a life for a self-confessed fabriholic and thread junky!

Janice Averill— Inspiration & Design

Ever since I bought the book *Rose of Sharon: New Quilts from an Old Favorite*, I wanted to enter this competition. In the past, I'd won a few ribbons in local quilt shows, but I didn't think that I could swim with the "big fish." With Janice, I knew we could create something special.

This past Labor Day, I came across the entry for this year's contest. We knew it would be a challenge to complete the project on time but we decided to go for it anyway. I started by drawing the block to make myself more familiar with its components. This exercise will usually get the creative juices flowing.

I came upon a cigarette case that I'd found in a thrift shop that had a pretty wreath of day lilies etched on it. I had bought it figuring it would pay off someday as a source of inspiration and indeed it did. The motif reminded me of a kaleidoscope or mandala and I decided to proceed in that direction. Traditionally there are three flowers in a Carolina Lily block, so I replaced each individual flower with three flowers and I liked the result.

I love the relationship of the colors in this quilt. Each complements its neighbor beautifully. I only started sewing this together the last week of September and Janice and I finished in time without making ourselves crazy. I love the way it came together so naturally. That's why Janice and I decided to call it ZEN LILIES.

With Electric Quilt® software I have been able to develop my color sense and my understanding of value. I don't have to use my precious fabric to experiment with color and fabric. Instead I use paper and ink. I create virtual quilts in EQ and print them out in black and white to see the relationship of the values in the design. If something isn't working you'll see it instantly in a greyscale representation of your design. I can also sort my fabrics by value in this way. Both strategies have been helpful in educating myself about color theory.

Janice Averill—Technique

Drafting a design and a master pattern

I usually design quilts with my Electric Quilt software, but this time I depended on paper and ink. I drew my original sketch on graph paper, so it wasn't difficult to maintain the proportions from the original sketch in the final pattern. I recommend a graph paper pad as a sketch book to all quilters.

I sketched the finished design on a new, larger piece of graph paper. I drew it at quarter scale. I worked out the design bugs until I was happy and then I created the master draft of the design. The pattern pieces were traced or measured from the master draft.

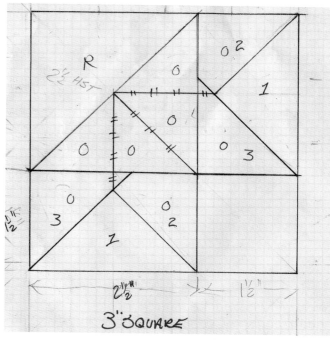

Freezer-paper foundation piecing in general

I latched onto foundation piecing very early in my quilting life. I love the precision it offers. *The Experts' Guide to Foundation Piecing* edited by Jane Hall (C&T Publishing, 2006) is a great reference. It describes many different foundation-piecing techniques used by many of today's top quilt designers.

I love to use freezer paper because the fabric from the previous step stays in place as I attach the next piece of fabric. I like to sew through the seam line because I feel it increases my accuracy without stressing my eyes trying to sew exactly next to the fold. I used this technique for the triangle-shaped wedge that contained the lily leaves. I also used it to piece the lily petals.

Avoiding Y seams with half-square triangles (HSTs) and foundation piecing

I wanted to avoid Y seams because of the small size of the flowers and the short amount of time we had to get this quilt done. I decided to draft the petals with what I call tall flying geese. I drafted the lily with the Y seams and then erased all the inside lines, leaving only the outline. I then converted the base/body of the flower to a HST. Next I drafted the petals units by simply continuing one line to the edge of the HST. I made freezer-paper patterns of this unit. After the petal units were done, I trimmed them and removed the paper. They were now ready to become a part of the finished Carolina Lily block.

Construction

The basic unit for this design is a kite-shaped wedge. To break down the parts for construction, I chose to create two subunits: the top flower unit and the bottom leaf unit. The bottom leaf unit was then divided into two units down the center. These were then broken down into smaller units that each contained a leaf. The leaf units were constructed using foundation piecing. The flower unit was also divided into smaller units and constructed using traditional machine piecing.

Janice Roy—Quilting the Quilt

Janice provided us with a sketch of a border design she envisioned when she designed the quilt. When we met to begin planning the quilting, I borrowed one of her resources for inspiration— *Pictorial Archive of Lace Designs: 325 Historic Examples* by Carol Belanger Grafton (Dover Publications, 1989). I studied the many different lace designs to look for connecting patterns to fill the background around the border designs and behind the flowers. Janice requested angular lines around the leaves to highlight the angle of the leaves in the center of the quilt. Mark scanned the design and digitized the pattern using AutoSketch® drafting software by AutoDesk to engineer the patterns that drive the Statler Stitcher system.

The border motifs are the only designs computer driven in this quilt. I free-motion quilted the remainder of the piece.

To prepare to quilt the piece, I mounted muslin on Yang and ran the new digital patterns of the border design and then doodled around the design until I found the stitching that I felt worked around the flowers and border designs. Then I mounted the quilt, selected the thread colors needed to complement the top, and completed the quilting. I quilted the border patterns across the top and bottom of the quilt along with the quilting in the center, then unpinned and remounted the quilt to do the borders along the sides. I feel they come out more evenly spaced if I can run them in one continuous line.

I like the weight and softness of a piece finished with Quilters Dream Cotton® Select Batting. I prefer Maxi-Lock® thread because it is light enough to prevent the finished project from feeling stiff, even if it is heavily quilted.

Finalists
Denver Electric Quilters

Denver, Colorado

Front row, left to right: Mary Leeper, Lynda Milligan, Ann Petersen, Barb Gardner
Back row, left to right: Judy Ahlborn, Katie Wells, Joan Christopherson, Terri Scott, Christine N. Brown

Chris Brown, Castle Pines, Colorado

My interest in Electric Quilt® design software began in the 90s when I hired a tutor to come to my home to teach me the program. I realized that working alongside someone else at the computer was a more effective way of learning for me than slogging through the manual solo. About four years ago, after taking EQ classes at quilt shows and online and still not making much progress, I decided to put out a call through local quilting friends to find other EQ fans who might want to form an EQ self-help "bee." The result is this amazing group of diverse but focused computer devotees whom I now call friends.

Our members decided that meeting twice a month would keep our skills sharp and knowledge current. The meetings last no longer than two hours, and we each bring laptops loaded with EQ7 and our projects installed. There is no group leader; with nine members possessing varying degrees of EQ skills, there are always questions to discuss and new ideas to be tossed around. We learn from each other. Some of us are better at appliqué, some at piecing, and some at designing, so there is plenty of knowledge to share. We also assign ourselves homework each meeting. The assignments are chosen as a group and vary in scope and difficulty. After working independently at home, each member then shares her sketchbook, design process, and final results on her laptop at the meeting while others observe.

As the retired editor-in-chief of the AQS publication *American Quilter* magazine, I was aware of the annual New Quilts from an Old Favorites contest and suggested that we each design an original Carolina Lily block as one of our assignments. We easily progressed to working together on an original setting for our blocks, and then decided to take the leap to fabric. Many obstacles popped up along the way, any of which could have derailed the project for a less dedicated group. But we persevered. (RADIANT BLOOMS is our second completed group quilt.) Every design and sewing decision was made as a group, amazingly with almost no disagreement.

Judy Ahlborn, Littleton, Colorado

Being the newest member, I feel lucky to be a part of such a wonderful and talented group of ladies who share my interest in using software as an essential design tool. Having an upbringing in art and sewing along with a career in computer technology, my PC has become an important part of my design process.

I like to create kaleidoscopes that I edit and enhance in Adobe Photoshop software, then import into Electric Quilt to create some of my quilt layouts. I oftentimes use two or three different programs to create my final designs, and have shared these ideas and my finished works with our group.

RADIANT BLOOMS

62½" x 62½"

While playing EQ catch-up with the rest of our group, I challenged myself to create some quilt layouts. In the process, I created the overall layout that eventually became the structure for our RADIANT BLOOMS quilt. Essentially, my circular quilt design became the frames into which our individual quilt block designs were fit. With just a few layout modifications along the way, we agreed on a final design.

Barb Gardner, Louisville, Colorado

Using Electric Quilt software to generate a quilt block or layout allows me to randomly play with shapes and ideas and create a final plan for an original work. Virtual quilting is so much faster and easier than paper and pencil. It's simple to mirror images, rotate, add lines, recolor, etc., and end up with a block or quilt I never would have dreamed up on paper or a design wall. This is what happened with RADIANT BLOOMS.

Each individual's block design was limited by the space between the arc and the block edges— basically a quarter-triangle shape. We each designed a flower inspired by the Carolina Lily to fit that shape. We laid out all our designs and picked the ones that fit together well, using a variety of techniques and good color flow.

The unique layout for the design was selected after we all brought in ideas. Through careful selection of color and shapes, we were able to blur the lines and add depth. Hopefully we have the viewer asking, "How did they do that?"

When it came to translating the design to fabric, challenges arose. Finding a color scheme all agreed to took several meetings. Then we had to shop for batik fabrics to bring our design to life. The block designs have arcs that have to fit exactly, with many points to match and the extra challenge of nine people sewing the blocks.

Lynda Milligan,
Westminster, Colorado

Early last February, our group headed south to the Hideaway Inn Retreat Center on the edge of the Black Forest, just north of Colorado Springs. Since we would all be together, we decided it would be a perfect time to get started on the quilt. We came prepared with our background fabrics, the black and white for the Sawtooth arcs, our original lily patterns, and an assortment of fabrics that we thought would look great in our blocks.

We also thought it would be a perfect time for Ann (Petersen) to teach us her award-winning method for paper piecing using freezer-paper templates. It was my responsibility to make a true, cleaned-up arc pattern and send it to Ann so that she could prepare the templates for each of us before she flew in for the retreat.

We settled into our bedrooms, set up our sewing spaces in a lovely spacious room, and ate a wonderful dinner. After dinner, Ann gave us a demonstration of her technique with which you never sew through your template, so there is no need to rip out paper after you have stitched.

Katie was the first one finished. She had come prepared with one of her Lily blocks already stitched. She attempted to fit the arc to her pattern and couldn't figure out why it wasn't fitting. After some confusion and a little measuring, the arc block was deemed too small. It was perfect for a 9" block, but a bit too small for a 10" block. We toyed for a bit on resizing all of our blocks to fit the arcs—but luckily we came to our senses before doing so.

I knew that I drew it up the correct size, but did I send the correct size to Ann? Ann also wondered what went wrong, but blamed the inaccuracy on using a printer that she wasn't comfortable with. Anyway, we all had a good laugh and chalked it up to a "unique" learning experience. As the evening wore on, we contributed our too-small arcs to this masterpiece.

We thought about making this into the label, but fortunately decided that maybe we should keep this to ourselves—so much for that!

The next morning, after a good night's sleep, we each laid out our patterns and the fabrics we thought would look good in our blocks on the backgrounds. We eliminated some, added and exchanged others, and came up with a wonderful palette. We discussed the best ways to make our blocks. A novice sewer, Terri was a bit hesitant to make a block and instead became our EQ guru.

She took all of our blocks and the layout and put together a complete and accurate rendition of the quilt and the individual blocks. This wasn't an easy task, as we had all designed a block with the EQ7 software in quite different ways. Her job was to make sense of how we accomplished the final design.

At the end of our three day retreat, we packed our

belongings, discussed what were the next steps in the process, and left refreshed and nourished with food, friendship, and creativity! What a wonderful weekend!

Katie Wells, Denver, Colorado

I came to this group a year and a half after it started, so I felt pretty intimidated. But with a lot of work and help from the group, I was able to design blocks for our first big "real quilt" project, PEPPERMINT PIZZAZZ.*

Our next project was this contest quilt. Two of my block designs were chosen by the group for this quilt. In designing my first block, I decided I wanted a close-up look of what a Carolina lily would look like, so I used the drawing tool in the EQ program and just started to play with the design. Since this was a drawn design, it had to be appliquéd. We decided on hand rather than machine appliqué. But since I don't do that very well, Joan did my appliqué and I did extra paper piecing of the arcs, which I love. For my second block, I found a Lily block in the EQ library. I manipulated the original design to make it my own. Since this block had straight lines, I decided to paper piece the block.

I have really enjoyed being part of this group as it has forced me to think outside the box. We have all benefited and learned so much from everyone.

Terri Scott, Aurora, Colorado

My contribution to the quilt was working with the EQ7 files and combining everyone's final blocks into a master file. There are many lessons to be learned when working with blocks electronically designed by eight other quilters. Some blocks were drawn in Easy Draw mode and some in EQ Patch Draw, and the two cannot be combined. But since our blocks all included the same Sawtooth arc designed in Patch Draw, I had to make many adjustments and redraws for everything to fit correctly.

I recommend that group members agree to

*PEPPERMINT PIZZAZZ is published as a series pattern beginning in the March 2014 issue of *American Quilter* magazine.

design in the actual size of the block to be used in the quilt. Some designed in a 6" block versus the 10" size used for the quilt. Normally this is not an issue. But when one part of the block is identical (the arc) for all blocks, it's hard to go from a 6" to 10" with a preset 2" arc. We also all made small adjustments when actually sewing our blocks. It would have been helpful if each person had made the appropriate changes in EQ7 immediately after making the block rather than months later, trying to remember what changes were made.

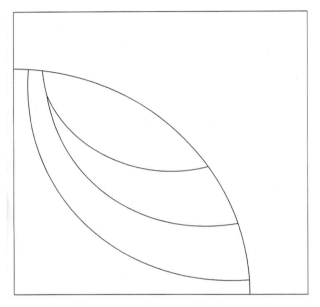

The leaf was redesigned by Chris Brown in the course of making the quilt to eliminate multiple seams at the block intersections.

Mary Leeper, Lakewood, Colorado

This contest quilt gave me an opportunity to design a block using a photograph and to create a paper-pieced block. The process of making a quilt block using a Carolina lily as my focus allowed me to learn more about importing a photograph into EQ to trace. I experimented with many pictures because my goal was to show the different colors on both the front and back of a petal. Another goal was to make a foundation pattern for my block in EQ. It took some experimentation and practice to make my pattern, and now I want to practice this skill on future blocks. I love making foundation

patterns! By working together, we learn from the program, the EQ books, and each other's discoveries.

Joan Christopherson, Centennial, Colorado

I started quilting in 1976—the year of the Bicentennial when quilting was just starting to pick up again. I took lessons from Lynda (Milligan) and she taught us everything from hand piecing to hand appliqué. We made a 12-block sampler quilt and, of course, mine was red, white, and blue. Over the years I retained my interest in quilting, even though I was not able to sew as much as I would have liked because of my job.

My first EQ program was EQ3. I was fascinated by the possibilities but did little designing. By the time EQ7 came out, I had retired and wanted to learn more about the program. I was thrilled when Chris Brown announced she wanted to start an EQ group. I thought it would be the perfect opportunity to hone my skills.

My block was drawn in the Patch Draw/Easy Draw mode and it was a challenge to make the appliqué fit inside the arc. The fun part was the hand appliqué of the block and choosing colors to make my block a part of the whole. Both our group quilts seem to showcase our individual talents.

The group has several highly talented quilters who have forced me to push my boundaries. With RADIANT BLOOMS, I took my love of appliqué and designed my block. I'm excited our quilt was chosen to be part of this exhibit.

Ann Petersen, Aurora, Colorado

I thought the overall setting design we worked on was dynamic, and I enjoyed designing several Lily blocks for the group's consideration. Though I was out of town at the time of final block selection, the group decided to repeat my block four times, radiating around the center on yellow fabric.

Because I knew I would be quilting the final quilt, I began thinking of many ways to quilt it even in the very early design stages. In the end, quilting designs that added entirely new elements to the quilt were rejected because of the busyness of the batik fabrics and complexity of the overall design. Drawing from the leaf motifs in some of the batiks, I quilted an overlay of veins on the pieced leaves in the quilt and then used similar quilted leaves with the same vein structure in the concave areas beneath each lily.

The petals of each flower were quilted with various flowing lines to emphasize the shape of the lilies. In the black-and-white spiked arcs, I decided to quilt a "shadow" set of spikes using electric blue thread. Each spike was drawn with a template of the same size as the white spikes, then each was echoed approximately ½" away and filled with a ribbon candy quilting motif. This ribbon motif was also used to create arcs in the blue background. The background was quilted with four different alternating filler designs to give both variety and cohesiveness to the quilt.

I do my quilting on a BERNINA domestic machine with a standard size bed. I especially enjoyed quilting this quilt and thinking about each person's contribution as I worked on their blocks.

RADIANT BLOOMS label

Radiant Blooms

Designed and Made by
Denver Electric Quilters
November 2013
Machine Quilted by Ann Petersen

Denver Electric Quilters

Front, left to right: Mary Leeper, Lynda Milligan,
Ann Petersen, Barb Gardner
Back, left to right: Judy Ahlborn, Katie Wells,
Joan Christopherson, Terri Scott, Christine N. Brown

Finalist
Sherri Bain Driver
Northglenn, Colorado

Photo by Mellisa Karlin Mahoney

Meet Sherri

My mother taught me to sew when I was just eight years old, but I remember being interested in fabric long before that. Mom and Grandma were both prolific seamstresses and they saved most of their scraps. When I visited Grandma, I would play with her fabrics, sorting them into color families, so it was no surprise to my family that I eventually stitched those scraps into quilts. At first I didn't know anything about making quilts, but I knew how to sew clothes, so I forged ahead making several horribly boring and ugly quilts! I eventually found a quilt shop, a guild, and quilty friends, and I became excited to learn all about quilting. It was life-changing.

In the following years I learned so much about designing and making quilts. I loved it! I became very active in a small guild and started teaching at the local quilt shop. Quilting has opened the door for a wonderful career for me. Over the last 15 years I've worked as an editor for several quilt magazines.

I am especially drawn to woven stripes and ikats. Ikat fabrics have patterns or designs dyed into the yarns before the fabric is woven. Some patterns are simple, subtle color changes along the warp or weft; others have very intricate motifs with patterns dyed in both the warp and weft yarns. I have a large closet full of these beautiful fabrics and I hope to use all of them in quilts.

Inspiration & Design

I love the NQOF contest and try to make a quilt for it each year. The contest has inspired me to try new sewing techniques and to expand my design skills. I don't always get a quilt completed for the contest, but I always design something, and that's half the fun. I started this quilt quite late in the summer, giving myself very little time to finish it by the contest deadline. As with most of my quilt designs, this one began as a rough sketch on graph paper. I really didn't have a color scheme in mind, but I just had to get started and hoped I'd become excited enough to continue.

I began by making the blossoms, choosing a red, orange, and yellow ikat with a bold design. I drafted a diamond to fit the fabric's woven motif, then I drafted the rest of the block around those diamonds. A brown print with dots and squiggles of brighter colors seemed like a good background and I selected a Kaffe Fassett woven stripe for the calyxes and stems. To keep moving ahead, I

LILYPALOOZA

62" x 62"

constructed the flower sections before choosing the rest of the fabrics for the quilt. Once those sections were made I came to a bit of a standstill. There were so many good fabric choices in my stash to add to the flower sections that I hardly knew which way to go. Perhaps naming the quilt would give me a direction.

I have no particular affinity to lilies, so that didn't help me name the quilt. Then I tried playing with the word, and eventually came up with LILYPALOOZA. That name seemed to beg for fun, lively colors and patterns, so I pinned some brighter stripes to my design wall to expand the color range. When purple was added to the other fabrics, I loved what I saw! Now I was ready to continue.

Fabric selection, in progress

I followed the design I had drawn, auditioning fabrics on the design wall and making additional parts as fabric choices were made. I hadn't worked out all the construction details beforehand, but kept making the sections and pinning them to my design wall. When it came time to assemble the top, I had to sew a lot of partial seams and mitered corners to get it all together!

I tried to keep the lively theme going with the quilting designs. I used some metallic and variegated threads to quilt a variety of designs, including freeform feathers and flowers with crazy petals.

Technique:
Simplified Set-In Seams

I never made a Carolina Lily block before I started this quilt, but I've made plenty of Eight-Pointed Stars that have the same shape diamonds and set-in patches. There are lots of techniques for sewing set-in seams and I believe I have tried them all! I have become most comfortable with the following method, which holds the diamond inner seams open to distribute bulk, while allowing flexibility in pressing the diamond/background seams.

I sew diamonds into pairs, starting from the raw edges of the points that will be at the star center, backstitching ¼" from the end of the seam where a background triangle or square will be set in; I press this seam open. I join the diamond pairs in the same way, starting from the inner (center) points, backstitching ¼" from the end of the seam, and pressing this seam open, too.

When setting in the triangular and/or square background patches, I sew with the diamonds on top. Insert a pin through the wrong side of the diamond's finished point (the exact point where the ¼" seams should intersect), then poke the pin through the right side of the background triangle or square at its finished point or corner. Pin the end of the seam in the same way, pinning through both patches to align the exact place where the seam should end. Align the raw edges and finish pinning securely, keeping the diamonds' seam allowances open.

Starting the seam at the diamond raw edge (not at the pin), stitch to the final pin, right across the open seam allowance. Stop with the needle down, piercing just one or two threads of the first diamond. Keeping the needle down, raise the presser foot and pivot the patches to align the edges of the second diamond with the underneath background patch. Using a stiletto or tweezers helps with the pivoting. Pin to align the finished point of the diamond with the finished point or corner of the background patch. Begin sewing the second edge, making sure the first stitch pierces one or two threads of the second diamond. Complete the seam, stitching all the way to the raw edges of the patches.

This method of setting in background patches allows some freedom in pressing subsequent seams.

Finalist
Nancy Eisenhauer
Belleville, Illinois

Photo by Gerard Reuter

Meet Nancy

I feel as though I stand on the shoulders of the quilters in my family who have come before me. I have handwork from two of my great-grandmothers. I remember my maternal grandmother always keeping her hands busy. She crocheted and quilted. Whenever we went to the farm, she would proudly show Mom and me her latest efforts. About once a year she would complete a bed quilt that would make the rounds of local fairs the next year. She had a drawer full of ribbons. How I wish I could share my work with her!

My dad was an expert woodworker. As he would show me his latest project, he would caress the wood the same way I "pet" fabric. He loved spending time in his workshop the same way I love to be in my studio. I guess what I'm saying is that this love of quilting, and the ability to creatively work with fabric, is in my DNA.

I have sewn since I was a child, but didn't move to quilting until I retired from teaching school in 2006. It has become my passion. I have met lots of caring, talented quilters and count many of them as my friends. Joining a quilt guild transformed both my technical skills and breadth of design. I have learned so much from other members and from the knowledgeable speakers and teachers our guild brings to us.

I find inspiration in travel, art, fabric, and even traditional quilt blocks. Traditional quilt blocks are a treasury of geometric design. There is always something new to be done by rearranging blocks or skewing all or part of a block. I try to make sure I have a camera with me whenever we travel, even if it is just a day trip. Usually I photograph textures and patterns in nature, textiles, and architecture. Art and other museums are full of beautiful examples of creative use of line, color, and space. Sometimes a trip to a good fabric shop or an interesting vendor at a quilt show will provide an idea for something new.

The past two years, I have had less time for quilting. My mother has had health issues that have demanded a lot of time and attention. I have tried to find handwork projects that I can take along to doctor appointments or work on while sitting in a hospital room. I have found that quilting can be a refuge—a place that takes me away from other problems and worries by demanding my full attention for a time. I have also found that there are times during which I can't put aside the thoughts in my head, and those are times for prayer rather than quilting. This quilt took about a year and a half from concept to finish. There were periods during which I didn't work on it for a couple of weeks at a time.

I love the quilting journey I have started. I don't know where it will lead, but I plan to enjoy the ride. As one of my favorite sacred anthems states, "The journey is my home."

Inspiration & Design

I have been looking forward to working with the Carolina Lily block in this challenge for several

LILIES FOR MARY

57" x 65½"

years. There is something about the simple floral design that begs to be elaborated. Grouping blooms, or using the elegant curves to create something else entirely, is a visual adventure. I like to work in circular designs. They create movement and interest. Picture a field of wildflowers blowing gently in the breeze. The stems gracefully bend as the air passes over the face of each bloom. The waves of bobbing flower heads seem to be friendly nods from Mother Nature. I knew this was at least part of the image I wanted in my quilt.

As I researched various pieced and appliquéd blocks with "Lily" included in the name, I found some very simple appliqué shapes that could be easily adapted to the design taking shape in my head. I soon realized that I was going to need more than some simple blooms in a circle. A stem with multiple blooms would help. How about more than one circle of blooms? How about overlapping circles of lilies? How about changing the scale to make it seem as though the circles of lilies are receding into the background? All those ideas appealed to me. Now the plain background I had planned bothered me.

I have a copy of Norah McMeeking's book, *Bella Bella Quilts: Stunning Designs from Italian Mosaics* (C&T Publishing, 2005) I have enjoyed simply looking at her work as she interprets the gorgeous mosaics found on those ancient cathedral floors in Italy. Each time I paged through the book, I would think, "Someday . . ." Well, the day arrived. I decided that what those blooms needed was an Italian cathedral floor on which to rest. An image that came to mind was that of flowers I had

seen placed on Princess Grace's resting place on the floor of St. Nicholas Cathedral in Monte Carlo, Monaco. The combination of delicate flowers and stone stuck with me. Using some elements of Norah's beautiful circular quilts, I designed three medallions in different scales. The uniting element for the medallions is the beam of light running from upper right to lower left of the quilt. I love to use color value to create the illusion of light and dark.

At this point I began construction. As is almost always true of my quilts, the entire design doesn't reveal itself all at once. I have to keep listening to the quilt. It will tell me what it needs. The medallions did not cover the entire surface of the quilt. I still needed a background. Having covered most of the quilt with intricate design, a plain background still didn't seem to work. Having looked at both pieced and appliquéd blocks for inspiration, I decided to use pieced blocks for the background. It was important to keep the contrast subtle in those blocks so they would stay in the background.

Naming my quilts is part of the fun. Usually this is fairly easy for me. Sometimes I have the title before the design. This quilt was stubborn about being named. I couldn't settle on a name. During the construction, a dear quilting friend, whose children I had taught in school, died. After seeing one of my first attempts at an art quilt, she had told me, "You are good. You need to enter these in something before you decide you are not good enough." I took her advice. After her death, I knew this was a way to honor her and celebrate our friendship—LILIES FOR MARY it is.

Technique

LILIES FOR MARY is a combination of construction techniques. The background blocks and medallions are pieced and foundation pieced. The lilies themselves are machine appliquéd.

The first part of construction was transforming the large, empty circles on my full-sized pattern into the medallions. I knew I wanted three different designs in three sizes. I started with circular grids printed from the Internet. By connecting points on the concentric circles within a given wedge, I created a design for one-eighth of a medallion. I transferred the design to freezer paper, enlarging it to the desired size. I traced the repeats on the paper side of freezer paper. I like doing large foundation piecing on freezer paper. The pieces stay put when pressed to the wax side of the paper.

As you look at the finished quilt, you can see that some of the wedges are crossed by the "sunbeam" on the quilt. I made two copies of some of the wedges or the needed portions—one in the light and one in shadow. The two were cut and attached along the appropriate line.

Finding fabrics that read the same color and texture but with different values (lightness or darkness) was sometimes a challenge. Thanks to a class I took from Katie Pasquini Masopust, I had worked with as many as seven values of a given color. For this project, it was also critical that I match the texture of the fabrics so that each medallion appeared to be one surface with light shining across it. There was a great deal of trial and error. Choosing from the fabrics scattered on the floor of my studio, I first glued fabric pieces to each medallion design in both light and dark areas. Upon sewing these fabrics into the wedge, I found that some worked and some didn't. Sometimes it was the transition to the lighted area that didn't work. I think I did more "unsewing" in this quilt than any I have ever done.

Once the medallions and partial medallions were completed, it was time to add the lilies. I modified an appliqué design I found and made copies in lots of sizes. Love those copy machines! The lily motifs had to be large enough not to get lost on the medallions, but not so large that they took over the surface. I tried assorted color combinations and techniques before deciding to do the lilies in red, orange, and purple using raw-edged, fused, machine appliqué. Once again, finding the right colors for the light and shadow areas was important.

At this point I finally decided to use an open lily, face-on, to finish the center of each medallion. Those motifs were hand appliquéd into place. I carefully cut and appliquéd the light and dark sections of each medallion together and then sewed all three medallions together. The blocks in the background were added last.

I didn't want binding on the edge of the quilt, especially since the lower right corner was one of the medallions. The solution was to do a knife-edge finish. That meant that the three layers of the quilt had to be sewn together and the quilt turned before doing any quilting.

I find quilting the most difficult part of what I do, so I worked in many short sessions. I quilted the surface from the bottom up, trying to stay fairly even across the quilt as I went. Finally, I reached the top and celebrated!

MILLEFIORI

73½" x 56½"

Inspiration & Design

I am fascinated with stripes. I love the force-field stripes create. They reach out, like fingers, like branches; they pulsate across the gaps between them. Stripes are just the most exciting pattern one could possibly use! They look terrific framed with solids, against which they vibrate all the more intensely.

The trio of flowers in the Carolina Lily block intrigued me—the way the leaves point in toward each other and the blossoms point out with bristly electricity. I used stripes in the blossoms and the leaves to represent the forces of growth, analogous to the veins that carry the plant's energy. I wanted to work with just the three LeMoyne Stars of the Carolina Lily block, with their six "flower" diamonds and two "leaf" diamonds.

I can never get enough of the glowing flow that results when colors are shaded in close steps. A color becomes a direction, a force, a motion, an emotion when it is part of a shaded group—not at all static. I sequenced all three elements of the threesomes. The backgrounds are shaded; so are the flowers; the leaves are sometimes shaded, but sometimes not (to hold the threesome together).

At the very beginning, I use graph paper to sketch ideas. My first attempt was to stack the V-shaped threesomes into vertical braids, with striped fabric between the braids.

Not pleased with that arrangement, I tried the V shaped threesomes in horizontal bands.

I began to develop long chains of closely related colors, which gave me more blocks to work with and more hints of the possibilities of interweaving them.

I realized that the threesomes would tessellate (interlock in a repeating pattern). I made a drawing with the tessellated triads pointed up and down.

I turned the drawing and saw that the threesomes could push left and push right. Diagonally left and diagonally right! Ah, yes!

Then I really had something I thought would be dynamic. I started interweaving the color groups, taking reds to the right and greens to the left.

Through the summer and fall, I worked on resolving the composition and the color into something coherent but not boring, varied but not fragmented. The challenge in quiltmaking is to allow a quilt to have its dazzling complexity, its endless dance of patterns, yet keep a structure that is clear, dynamic, and has unity. It's the big shapes and the big forces that command attention, not the details.

Shapes and colors, if I work hard enough, become embodied with emotion. There are quiet colors, loud colors, sighing colors, and shrieking colors; harmonizing colors and conflicting colors; soothing progressions or abrupt ones; jagged shapes or gentle fogs; plunging abysses or assertive planes. I didn't think of literal lilies or a literal garden, rather of abstract shapes and of an ideal garden.

Searching for a title (and running title ideas past friends), I was thinking about profusely multiplying flowers and polychromatic color. I thought of *millefiori* paperweights, which cluster tiny concentric flowers in a glistening glass globe. I have one of these paperweights, which had been buried in a closet. I found it, took it out, and was delighted to see it again. In its honor I settled on MILLEFIORI, which means "a thousand flowers;" a contained, controlled, riot of color; a fireworks of flower bursts; a paradise of seemingly infinite blossoms; an everlasting bouquet.

Technique

I use my domestic machine for quilting, and the thinnest loft of batting to minimize as much as possible the bulk that has to go through the machine. I use 50 wt. Aurifil thread for quilting (as well as for piecing). I'm never aiming for attention-getting quilting, since the color and design are of overriding importance to me, but I do aim to have the quilting integrate with the basic shapes of the composition.

I make a sample with leftover blocks to try out different quilting ideas. It's a bonus quilt, easy to compose after all I've learned with the "real" quilt.

I quilted quarter-circle curves that connect the flower centers. Because of the tessellated arrangement, the curves converge and diverge, converge and diverge. I used a flexible tape to mark the curved lines.

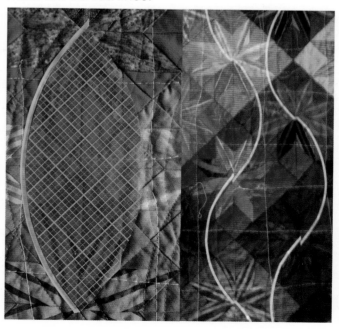

Finalist
Robin Gausebeck

Rockford, Illinois

Photo by Steven R. Gausebeck

Meet Robin

New Quilts from an Old Favorite and I are getting to be very good friends. This is my fifth year as a finalist and in 2011 my quilt ORANGE BLOSSOM SPECIAL won first place and graced the cover of that year's book. What a thrill!

Over the nine years that I have been quilting, my work has evolved and taken off in what seems like a million different directions. While I do not have a cohesive look that would identify a quilt as being mine, I have always been attracted to intense colors and my use of bright tones is common to most of my quilts. My style is definitely contemporary and I find inspiration in a variety of places. Frequently quilt titles pop into my head and my design notebooks have many more clever titles than I have time to turn into quilts.

Over the last couple of years, I have ventured into the world of miniature quilts. This has come as a bit of a surprise to me as I generally favor big, bold designs. However, I have become enamored of my very sharp scissors, tweezers, and BERNINA magnifier that enable me to design and construct machine-appliquéd quilts with lots of tiny pieces. In 2013, I was ecstatic when my miniature IN FLANDERS FIELDS won first place in its category at AQS QuiltWeek® – Paducah and second place at the IQA show in Houston. While these quilts are small, they seem to take me every bit as long to make as my much bigger quilts and present an entirely different set of design challenges. I guess when we stretch ourselves beyond what we believe we are capable of, interesting things can happen.

I continue to be amazed at the creativity of the annual NQOF finalists. Usually my first thought on seeing the quilts hanging in the museum is, "How did she/he ever think of that?" I look forward to the challenge of this contest and I now find myself thinking ahead several years to New York Beauty and Flying Geese, the 2016 and 2017 selections. The more time I have for brainstorming and reflection, perhaps the more creative ideas I can generate. I have to admit that I have a fun design for Nine Patch and have started sewing portions of it. New York Beauty is roughly mapped out in my head and Flying Geese, who knows? For many years, my husband has actually owned a small sailboat named Flying Goose. Maybe there's a nautical-themed quilt in my future.

Inspiration & Design

This contest has become a favorite of mine. There is no history of quilting in my family and I have never made a traditional quilt; rather, I leapt in as a contemporary quilter and have stayed there ever since. New Quilts from an Old Favorite, and the accompanying exhibit of antique quilts at the museum, has strengthened my respect for quilting's roots and challenge the way I think about design.

Carolina in My Mind

66" x 66"

My process for designing any of the quilts for NQOF has always begun with an extensive look at the history of each block and a review of quilts, old and new, that feature it. In this way, I can at least see how the block itself has changed over the years. It's amazing how contemporary some of the very old quilts appear in their design and color selections. By going through this process, I feel more connected to quilters of the past, even if none of them happened to be in my family.

Lately, I have been able to spend quite a bit of time with my three young grandchildren who moved last year to a house about a mile away. The oldest is four and often the first thing she says to me when she comes over is, "Grandma, can we go work in your studio?" While she is still a bit too young to sew on her own, she sits on my lap and helps me guide fabric. She has her own sewing tools and scissors and is learning to use them responsibly. She also has free reign among my scraps and likes to make glued constructions with bits and pieces of fabric that she calls her "quilts." She is particularly excited about my NQOF Nine-Patch quilt because her favorite number is nine and my design incorporates her favorite color, pink.

Critique Technique

I am especially pleased to be sharing space in this book once again with two people whose friendship I truly value. Karen Grover is my Rockford friend who offers unbiased critiques and great suggestions at our almost-weekly coffee and show-and-tell sessions. Karen Watts is my friend from far away whom I met because we both entered this contest the year of the Sawtooth block. We've been to shows and retreats together and I wish I could have coffee with her every week, too.

I have been in situations with both Karens where the give and take of constructive criticism has improved my ability to look at my designs with fresh eyes. Having someone whose ideas and objectivity you trust is invaluable in the design process. I think we have all heard stories about "Quiltzillas" who take every opportunity to point out what isn't up to par on a quilt. However, constructive critiques couldn't be more different.

There are several things to remember about making critiques useful:

- Criticism and critique are two different concepts. Please do not give unsolicited advice unless you know that it will be welcomed in the spirit in which it is intended. Karen Grover and I have regular show-and-tell sessions where the purpose is not only to share what we've done but to talk over ideas and try to solve problems.

- The entire point of constructive critique is to get to a better end product. Remember to share the joy when an idea works well.

- This is all about someone else's quilt, not yours, so try to understand her/his vision and keep suggestions within that context.

- Suggestions should always be phrased in a positive fashion. Don't say what might be wrong but offer an idea that enhances a quilt's look; for example, "What would happen if you used this color here instead?"

- When possible, share not only your ideas but your stash! If you have just the fabric that your quilter friend is looking for, give it gladly unless you are saving it for a specific purpose. We know that we all have more fabric than we can possibly use and if something you own will help enhance someone else's quilt, that's a good thing.

- You are never bound to follow someone else's advice but be open to the possibility that it is good advice and could make your own quilt better.

Finalist
Karen Grover
Rockford, Illinois

Photo by Phil Grover

Meet Karen

Four years ago I took a deep breath and entered a quilt in the American Quilter's Society Quilt Show & Contest show in Paducah. Little did I know that small leap would set me free to be fearless in entering contests. My first entry was accepted and I had another one accepted last year. I do a lot of needle-turn appliqué, so it takes a while to complete a quilt. I am currently working on a new design—appliqué again. I should have picked something that doesn't take so long, but I like to appliqué. I find it very soothing.

SOFTLY GROW THE LILIES is my third entry in this contest. I look forward to entering again and again. The New Quilts from an Old Favorite challenge pushes the edges of my patience with the creative process but forces me to explore different ideas, looking for the best design. This year's entry has no appliqué at all, but was a fun quilt. I have next year's design hanging on my board right now. Honestly, I hope it will be the one and only design. Doing six designs this year was a lot of work and was somewhat stressful, but ultimately a great exercise that resulted in a quilt I love.

Now that I am retired, I have time to play with designs and it is fun as well as rewarding. There are times when I wish I could just design something that wasn't so complicated. But I guess that is me—creative, complicated. I seem to have a love affair with the complicated, and as Rube Goldberg said, "Why make it simple when complicated is so much more interesting?" I keep thinking I would like to write a pattern or two, but

I am not sure I could deconstruct some of them into sane instructions. It looks like that could be my next big challenge!

Design Process

I love quilt challenges. They bring out ideas—the good, the bad, and the ugly. But even the ugly can turn into something magical when that "click" happens. The process of designing a creative Carolina Lily block proved to be one of the longest design processes I have ever had. It is one of my favorite blocks. I love the simplicity of it when I see it in antique quilts, and I have a simple quilt I made using the pattern and it still makes me happy. However, SOFTLY GROW THE LILIES is my sixth Carolina Lily design and so the story begins.

My first design got as far as drawing the appliqué full size. At that point, I made a couple of background blocks and instantly knew I didn't like it.

SOFTLY GROW THE LILIES

53" x 54"

On to design number two.

Quickly on to number three. I made small mock-ups of both of these and chose to work on number two. I got the background fabric, drew the full-size pattern, and began machine appliquéing the flowers. I had wanted a 60s look to the flowers and was pleased with the first one I did. When I stood back and looked at it, I thought maybe I should try something else.

Design number four was inspired by a screen saver on my computer. I liked the composition and did a drawing. I don't like to quilt crosshatching around appliqué. Because of this, my next bright idea was to make the entire background AND quilt it first. I marked the sandwiched background using crosshatching and a couple of designs transferred from parts of stencils. It was quite fun to quilt; no appliqué in the way! Parts of the appliqué flower

design came from my design number one. I also made a full-size pattern for this quilt.

After spending an entire weekend basting the appliqué onto the quilted background I stood back and looked at it and hated it. I don't think I have ever felt so bad about something. In spite of this, I gathered my feelings and gave it the old college try.

On to number five: I don't have a picture of this, but it was similar to Katie Pasquini Masopust's method of color blocking. About a week later, that one came down, too. I put everything away and went upstairs to tell my husband I was not entering this year. At the time, calling it quits was a relief. It had been quite a journey and I was glad to have made that decision.

Two weeks later design number six just happened. I have a lot of lilies in my garden and after taking some pictures, I wondered what would happen if I printed them on fabric and used them in a design. SOFTLY GROW THE LILIES came softly and grew rapidly. I love it when a design feels right. This one had no sketch, no full pattern for appliqué, in fact, no appliqué at all. It came from that place where all designs reside and manifested itself on my design wall section by section. What fun!

Making the Quilt

I have a notebook with pages torn from various magazines. It includes anything that catches my eye. One of the pictures was divided into uneven wedges. That is where this quilt started. I measured out 50" on my design wall and used yarn to mark off five wedges.

Printing pictures on fabric is easy if you have good freezer paper. I ended up using a roll of butcher paper that I had purchased by mistake instead of the standard freezer paper. It provided a much stiffer backing and seems to have a thicker layer of wax on it. I had no problem running it through our color printer. I cut sheets 8½" x 11" and ironed them on to a variety of random yellow to gold fabrics also cut to that size. The fabric was all cotton, some hand-dyed. By trimming the leading edge of each sheet just before printing on it, I was able to make sure that the fabric completely adhered to the butcher paper on that edge. I did flowers, stems, buds, and groups of flowers. I also made several traditional 4" Lily blocks to tuck into corners here and there. To give the traditional blocks a different look, I dug out some silk pieces and pieced them using both cotton and silk. I liked the contrast. I had some leftover woven silks my daughter had brought back from Thailand several years ago. Basically, these were added to whatever I could pull from my stash. Time to begin.

I placed the flower prints in different spots on my design wall. Then I placed the small Lily blocks, and finally I put the woven silk pieces in spots where I thought I might want some horizontal lines. It was easiest to work in small sections. I worked with them as you would a small quilt. When I was pleased with a section, I moved on to the one directly below it until I had each wedge complete. This continued across the quilt.

Trimming the wedges proved to be my next challenge. I fumbled with a couple of marking methods, but eventually I just cut. This was the scariest part of the process. I did need to adjust a couple of the wedges as I went along. Once they were together, I took a picture to see what needed to happen next. The green lines seemed to be just the right dividing line. They are there, but not too prominent.

The quilting was something that I had thought about all along. I knew I wanted to "sketch" on the quilt after I finished the main quilting, and I wanted the flowers to go outside the block if that was needed. Once done, it still looked flat. I got nervous again. I knew there would be no design number seven in this process. By adding the embroidered stamens and the crystals, I got the depth that the flowers needed and breathed a sigh of relief.

I hope my next entry will not be so tedious.

Finalist
Ann Holmes
Asheville, North Carolina

Photo by Ann Holmes

Meet Ann

Carolina Lily, a favorite quilt block, and the need for sunny thoughts after a cold, wet summer in Asheville were the motivation for answering this challenge. Demonstrating my NO Sewing Until You Quilt It technique in my vendor booth for the three days of the Asheville quilt show at the end of September would provide a nice chunk of time to work on the quilt.

In addition to being a quilter, I'm a stained glass artist. Many years ago, I made Carolina lilies in stained glass for my shower stall. The framing is still needed. It's on my husband's to-do list, but he is forgiven as he ended up sacrificing one of his Hawaiian shirts for this quilt.

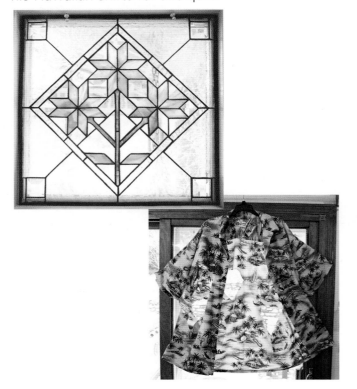

Inspiration & Design

First, I went to my stash of Hawaiian fabric that I bought there in 2005. I felt like I hit the jackpot when I found three yards of this screen print with boats: my mental escape to a warmer climate with palm trees, sand, sky, and water. What was I thinking when I purchased it eight years ago? Surely, I was not thinking of making my husband a shirt! I always buy fabric that I like—one of life's little pleasures. I am so grateful!

This is all that remains of that screen print. In the beginning, I was even thinking of using the pineapple border for the binding but later thought it was too busy.

Because my design is symmetric or nearly so, only half of the design was drawn full size. I built this quilt on top of my drawing with one continuous 60" wide square piece of French Fuse interfacing used as a foundation over the drawing. I built both halves of this quilt on top of the same

CAROLINA LILIES GO HAWAIIAN 52" x 52"

drawing, with that same wide piece of French Fuse, just by rotating the first half of the quilt 180 degrees and continuing to build the second half of the quilt. The second half was joined as I was building and I did have to make a few adjustments at the joining, but it worked.

For drawing the design, I used 36" wide butcher paper from a wholesale food supplier. To prepare my full-size sketch, I drew half of a 54" square, folded the paper in half to find the center point; opened the paper, then drew half of a 47" circle with a large compass. I centered one three-flower segment on the center line of the paper, tilting all flower heads to point toward the outside. I traced that flower unit and positioned the center flower on the right and left sides of the drawing, thereby drawing half of each unit on the right and left sides.

After getting the lilies properly spaced, I drew half of a center circle and softened the look of it to represent the center island as an anchor for the lilies. The lilies are spread out floating in the ocean, soaking up the sun. I wanted to give a relaxing, going-with-the-flow feel for the leaves. This fabric was the design inspiration and actual fabric used for the leaves.

The other islands are simply represented by sandy beaches and tropical foliage. The screen print of boats and palm trees used in large chunks for the four corners make the boats appear to be circling the islands.

I knew that I wanted the lilies to wear Hawaiian shirts and sunglasses. The shirts were easy. To give them a head or face, I drew one pointed petal on each flower. The sunglasses are from a photo I took as I passed a sunglasses display in a store. After reducing the size, I used Printed Treasures® fabric sheets to print them. The sunglasses and the hibiscus flowers were backed with Wonder-Under® fusible web. They are the only raw-edge pieces.

Finding time to work on this quilt at home was a challenge, so I worked on this quilt after traveling to Rhode Island to visit my daughter. I worked the original drawing on her dining room table. I used a lot of pencil, eraser, white out, and tracing and carbon paper. It was such a mess that I had to make a cleaner copy, and ended up taping 8½" x 11" copier paper together to make big paper.

Back in Asheville, I built the first half of the quilt, and then used the same freezer-paper patterns to cut fabric for the second half. This was in preparation for building the second half of the quilt while demonstrating at the Asheville Quilt Show.

Julie Bagamary was my assistant to demonstrate building CAROLINA LILIES GO HAWAIIAN and to help me as a vendor at the show. All projects in this booth are made with my technique.

After the show, I used 505® Spray and Fix adhesive to make the quilt sandwich and began to stitch and machine quilt at the same time using my straight-stitch Juki® machine. I work with invisible thread on top and 40 wt. rayon in the bobbin.

There would be no time to wash and block this quilt! I traveled to Missouri where I finished the stitching and quilting on my old BERNINA 1008 that I keep at my son's house. The binding was put on and then I realized that I forgot my good camera to take the photo to enter the competition! Luckily, my son had a new cell phone with an 8-mega-pixel camera!

My "NO Sewing Until You Quilt It" Technique

First, make a freezer-paper copy by tracing the original drawing. Place a layer of French Fuse over your original drawing. Use paper scissors to cut out the freezer-paper pattern pieces and place them on the French Fuse in their correct location; this makes fabric selection easy.

Iron the freezer-paper patterns onto the right side of your selected fabric! Working on the front of the quilt, you do not need to reverse anything. Add seam allowances to each pattern piece. With Ann's Magic Button, when you roll the button along the freezer paper edge you will have automatically added seam allowances. Place pattern pieces at least ½" apart and iron with a cotton setting—hot enough to hold onto fabric, but not too hot to melt wax from the freezer paper into the fabric.

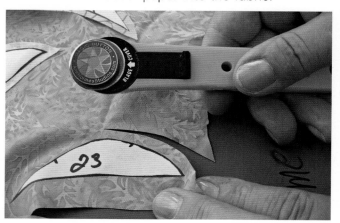

Build appliqué style from the background to the foreground. The first pieces are positioned by lifting the seam edges to see the lines underneath, then sealed down all over **including** the seam allowance, using a sealing iron. The first piece is done and you are ready to build around it. As you build, the seams will be overlapped.

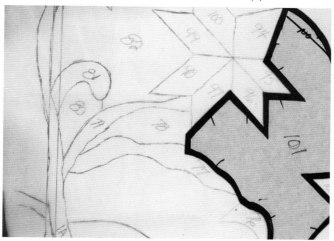

As you build, one piece at a time, hold the piece in position, and ask yourself, "Where will it touch?" As in hand appliqué, you turn only the edge or edges that will have a finished edge; the other seams are just left exposed, as a new piece will cover it as it is placed.

Here are the steps for turning edges:

1. Use glue stick on the backside of the fabric where you want to turn under the edge. I use a small cutting mat for gluing. It can go to the sink for washing when necessary.

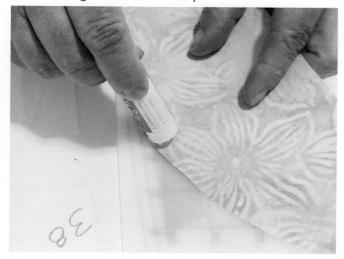

2. Have the freezer paper facing you to turn edges; use your hands to roll back the edge. Only inside curves need to be clipped for smooth turning.

3. Put the freezer paper face up and finger press along the turned edge. Finger pressing is the only pressing in the entire quilt top!

4. Keep everything flat, and clip off any dog-ears.

5. Glue the backside edges of the turned-under seam allowance. **Be generous with the glue. The glue holds the seam allowances together. The French Fuse holds the body of the quilt together until you do the stitching and quilting all at once.**

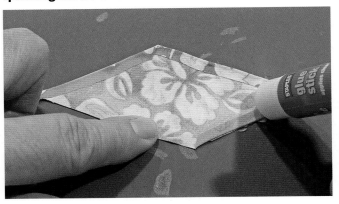

6. Seal in place, matching any registration marks. Here you can see the turned edges as you build without sewing.

TIPS: Keep your glue stick fresh in a shot glass with a damp paper towel or baby wipe in the bottom. I use a sewer's stiletto (seen behind the orange flower) for sliding under the freezer paper to remove it when no longer needed for positioning the next pieces.

AQS published Ann's book, *NO Sewing Until You Quilt It,* in June of 2012. See her website at: AnnHolmesStudio.com where she has a blog and an online store of the products she uses in her technique.

Finalist
Barbara Holtzman
Holyoke, Colorado

Photo by Joanie Groshans

Meet Barbara

Early on, my mom taught my sisters and me to sew. I sewed clothing for myself in high school. It was a good way to learn the basics. Although different from sewing quilts, it gave me a good background. Quilting started out as a pastime when my kids were both in college and I finally had some extra time of my own. It has developed into a creative outlet, a passion, and a way to memorialize events, people, and ideas. Quilts can be a piece of art—a memory of a time, place or event, or person. They are much more than a covering for a bed.

Having quilted fairly consistently since 2000, I have made it a point to try many different techniques. Now when I get ready to work on a quilt, I first work on the design and colors. Then I review my past skills and decide how I want to construct the quilt. All of this can change during the sewing process as I may discover a different or better way to get the job done.

I haven't taken as many classes as I would like to, being several hours from any major city. I have collected a variety of quilt books on all aspects of quilting, and often go to my library to give me ideas of color and design. Every other year I try to take advantage of Quilt Colorado and have been able to learn from very talented nationally known quilt teachers. I still work full-time, which competes for a lot of my time. By the time I get home from work, I'm usually too tired to do much of anything—even quilting! I try to fit quilting into a few minutes or an extended period of time, if possible.

I enjoy entering contests. I know they have helped me improve my skills, as I try to get better and better. I look forward to the judges' comments, good or bad, and try to improve because of them. I wrote QUILTS IN MY CUBICLE (AQS, 2008) which was a real challenge. It made me realize how hard it can be to write directions for quilting!

Inspiration & Design

One of the reasons I enjoy the NQOF contest so much is that it gives me a starting point and challenges me to come up with something new and creative. The fun is in taking that challenge and trying to put my own stamp on it.

We are all influenced by our environment and the people and events in our lives. The inspiration for the development of this quilt came from personal events in my life—in this case, the discovery that my younger sister had been diagnosed with cancer. In all trials, we go through a series of feelings. In my case it was probably pretty typical—denial, anger, fear, grief, acceptance. As I was working on this quilt, the act of sewing, pressing, and trimming was therapy for all the turmoil in my mind. I wanted to build a quilt that showed how while all of us go through different challenges in our lives, we can come out of them with a renewed sense of ourselves, a stronger inner self that we may not have known we have. Much depends on our outlook and how we can reach inside ourselves, build our faith, use our faith, and draw on the support of the people around us. My sister had such a positive attitude and determination. I truly admired her strength.

REBORN

79" x 79"

I had decided to make this quilt as large as the challenge allowed. The design went through several revisions. Yet, as I continued to doodle the design, the central theme stayed the same, showing the light and strength in of all of us. Originally the background was to be black, not blue. The colors in the star were to be more primary colors. I had made a mock star and petals with the black and primary colors. In fact, when I went searching for fabric, that's what I was looking for.

I was unable to find a black that seemed to fit with the idea I had in mind. Then, I found a wonderful hand-dyed mottled blue and decided to use it instead. That changed the other colors, since it seemed to require a different palette. I was going to appliqué flowers between the petals in the background. Even though I made the quilt as large as possible, my petals were large enough that I thought it would get too cluttered, and I took them out. At some point I hope to make a smaller version of this quilt, add the appliquéd flowers, and change the whole palette.

When I start a quilt and have an idea in mind, I pull out all my bins of fabric, one for each color. These hold the fat quarters or half-yard cuts. I have another area where I keep fabrics of larger amounts. I try to keep my stash to a minimum since I'm limited on space, occasionally challenging myself to use only those fabrics I have on hand. In this case, pretty much the only fabric I bought was for the background and the backing.

It's fun to use lots of different fabrics, watch how they work together, and create a design all their own. Since I like to use many different fabrics in a quilt, I don't usually need much of any one fabric. This can also be an advantage because when I do find fabric I like, I only buy about a half yard.

Sometimes I think I need to work on a more sophisticated palette, but eventually my color choices inadvertently come back to the saturated colors I love. Whether that is from the era I was raised in or not, I don't know, but I'm sure it has influenced me. Color has such an effect on us. I love color!

I fell in love with the Lone Star after a guild challenge. I usually don't enjoy working much with traditional blocks, but this was one that I have been almost obsessed with! It amazes me how the design changes with the placement of colors. The challenge quilt that I first worked with was a diamond that was only a 4 x 4 grid and had a limited color palette, yet so many different designs came out of it simply based on where colors were placed. The symmetry of the Star is very pleasing to the eye. Now I find myself searching for ways to include the Lone Star in a quilt!

The glow in the middle reflects the light and the determination we each carry inside ourselves. I quilted an outline of the flowers, stems, and petals in the dark blue background that mimic what is going on in the main flower, but are shadows of turmoil and dark times in our lives, many times under the surface.

Technique

I drew two large diamonds to size on a large sheet of paper with a 1" grid of 8 x 8 diamonds and put it up on my design wall. I didn't want the pattern in the diamonds to all be the same. I wanted to make four of each of the two diamonds, alternating them so the final look would be one of chance, not the perfectly symmetrical star that is usually made. I wanted the star to be more spontaneous, which ironically required more thought and time for placement and design.

I went through my stash of yellows, reds, oranges and pinks, cutting a lot of diamond pieces of the different fabrics. Taking one color at a time, I pinned each color to the paper diamond, randomly placing fabric with the goal being a glow from the center, turning warm on the outer edges. After I made my initial selections, I stepped back to get a view of what it was looking like. Pieces were exchanged or removed, until I was satisfied with the final result.

I needed to make some kind of master color grid chart to keep track of all the different fabrics. I redrew the two diamonds on a smaller scale on a piece of paper and, starting with the outside corner of one of the diamonds, I gave each individual fabric a number, writing that number down on my master color grid.

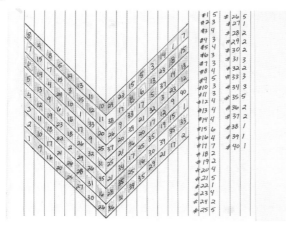

As I went through each fabric, I counted the number of times that a particular fabric was used in the two large diamonds and wrote it down to the right of the diamonds. This gave me the number of 1½" fabric strips I would need to cut. Since I had so many different fabrics, and some that also looked pretty similar, I also cut a square of each fabric, glued it to a different master sheet, and numbered it, tying it to the grid.

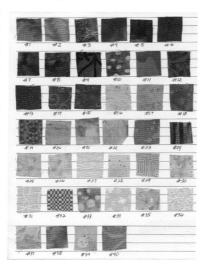

After I was happy with all my choices, I cut 1½" strips of however many that particular color needed. Each strip was about 14" long. I planned that this would give me some extra strips to use in the border (and it did!). Since I had 40 different fabrics, I used a drying rack to lay them out in the same order that I had numbered them. My fabric master helped keep order while I sewed. I offset the strips as I pieced them to allow less waste. I like to press my seams open. Each crossing seam needed to be basted before the final sewing. After I had all the strips pieced I laid them out to get an idea of how they would look.

The flowers, leaves, and stems on the large golden petals were raw-edge machine appliquéd. I used Wonder-Under to help keep the edges from fraying. All the edges were also button-hole stitched and later decorative stitching was applied to the petals.

Quilting was the final step. I've especially started to enjoy quilting feathers, so those are incorporated into some of the petals, along with free motion and stippling. Quilting becomes a calming, meditative process; and though I still am working on the quality of my quilting, I have improved and realize I won't get better if I don't practice!

Finalist
Tina McHenry
Jamestown, Pennsylvania

Photo by Cynthia A. Briggs

Meet Tina

The quilting journey for me has taken a huge turn in the past few years in that as an empty nester with two grown children, I am able to focus on my quilting every day. My original sewing space was the closed-in front porch of the farmhouse where we raised our children. It was a very bright room with windows all around, but very cold as it had no heat except a plug-in portable heater.

Several years ago my husband and I decided to build a new home on the property where he was raised. I designed the floor plan around my basement sewing studio where my leisure time would be spent. The best part of the room is the design wall/closet doors at the far end of the room, where I am able to see the projects develop. Prior to this, I would work on a project and lay it out on the floor; and of course the cat or dog would have to walk across it, or curl up in the middle.

Most mornings I am up and in my room by 5:00 a.m., designing and sewing and quilting on projects. Touching and working with the fabric is mental therapy, helping me to get through the long days at work. Few people understand the obsession of working on one quilt then another, with the dream of the next project never ending. Yes, there are many going at one time, and more than I would like to mention that are waiting for my return. Even though I finish several a month, there are always more new ideas fluttering around in my mind.

How thankful I am for the encouragement I receive from my family, friends, and coworkers.

They listen to my "crazy" ideas and are always willing to ooh and aah at my latest completed piece, at times offering to feed the ideas with a little "crazy" of their own.

Even though my husband, Dean, doesn't understand my need to sew, he is supportive of me; at times he waits for me to collect my items from a local fair, and helps me carry my treasures home.

There is a special friend who has inspired and fed my need to be more creative. Without Cindy (my headshot photographer), I wouldn't have come to be the quilter I am. We have taken so many wonderful trips with quilting always on our minds and on our itinerary. In our travels we have gone to many quilt shops, seen numerous quilt shows, and taken instruction from some of the best quilters in the world. Those days we spend creating together are so much fun and I look forward to many more.

Inspiration & Design

I look forward to working on challenge quilts. The process of creating something that is solely mine teaches me a great deal. This traditional quilter can be pushed and shoved into being the artistic creator of something totally my own, pushing me to a level I thought I could never and would never achieve. Originally, quilts had only one purpose: to keep someone warm. Look how far we have come.

In starting to look at the traditional Carolina Lily patterns, I realized that they were usually

The Seedlings

50" x 51¾"

a colored flower and stem on a solid white background. Lilies that grow in nature all come from a parent plant or root, so I created a tall lily with colored flowers and leaves. For me, that large colored plant represents the parent, the controlling entity of the family. We as parents are in charge of making children grow to be responsible, strong adults who can stand with the examples set by us.

The plain white lilies represent us as children. How small and seemingly insignificant we all start out! Each flower is as cute as the next one—very much the same, yet different in its own way. Growing only with love and nurturing, we become part of the big picture of family, neighborhood, and community. We grow with mentors and friends who encourage us to develop into good, healthy, creative, strong adults, always pushing past the limits set before us by others.

The difficult part of this challenge was to make the plants nest against themselves. I did not want to separate the seedlings from each other by sashing because they needed to be very close to each other. In nature, the individual plant is supported by its neighbor. They are individuals that spread out from the mother root. As a family/cluster of plants the roots grow together as a unit, not segregated by boundaries, dependent on each other's strength.

I was inspired to paint lilies in the border by a field of lilies that we visited last spring. We were on a girls' day road trip and stopped at Campbell Pottery. They weren't open yet and so to fill a few minutes we went next door to admire the lilies in the field. There were many different colors and sizes of lilies, all reaching for the sunlight.

Technique

To start, the lilies were created on graph paper—first the large mother plant, with her subtle colors of gold and green. Then, I began fitting in the small seedlings to form the surrounding plants.

They would be made from different cream-on-cream fabrics.

After deciding on the design, it was time to decide how big to make the quilt. The wall over my bed has two wall sconces on each side, and I would like to hang it there when it comes home. So it needs to be on the small side, less than 60" square. I figured if I made 1" finished squares, it would give me a nice border to play on and not be too big.

The fabric for the background had been picked from a batch of ice-dyed fabric that had been done at Cindy's house. She introduced me to hand-dyed fabrics and we have been playing with different methods of creating beautiful colored pieces ever since.

I began piecing in the bottom left corner, working at an angle from there. I used sticky notes to cover the areas on the drawing that were done so I didn't accidentally do the same part over again. This was my road map.

As I worked my way through the cutting and piecing, it was important to keep the various colors of the background flowing and visually appealing. Cutting the various flower petals and surrounding areas was sometimes confusing; and yes, I did get lost at times, occasionally ripping out something that didn't look quite right.

My mother was the one who would rip out when I was young, as it was something I despised; then I would resew. After I got older, I realized that she was right—if it isn't right I wouldn't like/love it and would always look at it as being wrong. When teaching friends, I have learned to say, "If it's good enough for you, then it's good enough for me." That is their signal that something isn't right, and they need to look closer. We are our own worst critics and sometimes that pays off.

During this process, I was considering quilting options, even though the piece wasn't even close to completion. I doodled quilting designs throughout the process. The repetition of drawing is how I practice for the quilting. Also this gives me many options when I do finish piecing, and am ready to quilt.

The painted lilies were applied with fabric paint after I had drawn them on with a fine white pencil.

I had allowed myself several inches bigger than the 50" size requirement, never imagining that I could quilt 2½" out of the finished size. Lesson learned! Next time I will leave myself at least 6" more than the smallest allowed measurement. I often make borders on wall quilts asymmetrical, giving the eye something different to focus on.

Claudia Clark Myers

Duluth, Minnesota

Photo by Thomas T. Myers III

Sewing Spaces I Have Loved

I am thinking about the sixty-seven years I have been sewing and the spaces where I have set up shop. Some were large, with good lighting and storage space, and some were small, "make-do" places, but, they all enabled me to enjoy one of my favorite occupations—making things with a sewing machine.

I remember being under the big wooden kitchen table where my mother set up her Featherweight when I was six. I was hand stitching two discarded sleeves together to make a pair of pants for my doll. When I was eight, my mother taught me to sew doll clothes on the old Singer® treadle. I can only remember running over my finger once. By the time I was in my teens I had gone from doll clothes to my own clothes.

My parents gave me a Singer® Futura™ machine for high school graduation. What a treasure! Three years later, when I married Tom, it went with me to Minneapolis while he finished medical school. It also went to Germany with us when Tom was in the Air Force. Our German landlady let me use a small room in the basement for my first "sewing room." There I made maternity and baby clothes.

Back in Rochester, Minnesota, in 1965, I took over a corner of the utility room in our residents' housing unit, as Tom finished his dermatology residency at the Mayo Clinic. I could only sew at night when the three little ones were asleep, but it was a lovely, warm nook, snuggled up to the furnace. I think that's where my night-owl tendencies come from.

The next move to Minneapolis saw me set up in a small basement room of our little English Tudor house by Lake Harriet. In 1969, we moved to Duluth and bought a huge, old Victorian house. I made great Halloween creations and hundreds of Minnesota Ballet costumes. I started my Victorian pillow business, Confections, and began my career in costume design and construction. Dealing with the more substantial fabrics used for costumes and millinery made it necessary to buy an industrial sewing machine, so my Singer® 20U became my new best friend.

Many Nutcrackers, Traviatas, Swan Lakes, and Carmens were churned out on that machine. I mostly worked for A T Jones & Sons, costumer, doing hats, headpieces, and principal costumes for the Baltimore Opera. I would do the construction in Duluth and then go to Baltimore for fittings and finishing. A T Jones & Sons was set up in an old, three-story brick warehouse on Charles Street. They used industrial machines that were so old they didn't even reverse, but they would sew through anything!

In 1990, Tom and I moved to 20 acres of north woods and built a beautiful log house. I designed and set up my dream sewing shop and took up quilting. My machines now numbered six or so, including several vintage BERNINAs. In 2001, I helped American Professional Quilting Systems develop George, a sit-down quilting machine, and was given the prototype which I still use. Many quilts came to life in that wonderful studio, and during those years, I became a quilt teacher, author, speaker, and (yay!) award winner.

LILYPALOOZA

68" x 72"

Now, we have moved back to town, and LILYPALOOZA is the first quilt I have made here, in my happy, yellow studio. I have discovered that if you truly enjoy doing something, you not only make time for it, but you find room for it, as well.

The Birth & Development of LILYPALOOZA

I really needed a quilt project! I hadn't touched quilt fabric for about eleven months, except to pack it up. Tom and I had spent the last year getting our log house ready to sell, finding a house in town that would work for us, and actually packing everything up and moving. We had lots of help from family and friends, but there had been no time for either of us to enjoy our avocations—he's a potter, I'm a quilter.

I love doing the NQOF challenge because it provides a starting point to work from, and I'm good with assignments. I compare it to the difference between decorating an empty, white room or decorating an empty, white room that has a red couch in it. You have a "given" to start with, and that works for me.

Wanting to do something different from the traditional block colors, I thought I would go with purple and orange. I started my design with a cartoon-like sketch of a lily on graph paper, making a somewhat folk art-looking design that also incorporated a chunk of the traditional pieced block.

I started paper piecing and appliquéing these blocks but the purple palette didn't even last through the first setting version. I went back to the traditional red and added black to ground it. The yellow adds continuity through the three different block designs.

After trying a medallion setting, plus several different versions of a horizontal strippy setting, I marched the folk art lilies through the middle, then around in a circle, and then cut them down to three. I finally settled on lining them up along the bottom, and adding the exuberant lily bouquet to top it off. The half circle of "traditional" Carolina Lily fans contributed some much-needed light, but they went through some changes, too.

They started out making a row through the middle. Then they were touching and making a huge arch at the top. Then there were three, then two, and finally back to five, but not touching, so there was some breathing room between them. Oh my! Too many choices!

Necessity finally made me stop rearranging, when I realized that there were only two weeks left before the deadline and I still had machine quilting to do. My husband, who also named the quilt LILYPALOOZA commented, "Sometimes you have to stop gilding the lily!" Ha, ha, ha! He was joking—but he was right.

The Technical Stuff

Most of you who quilt know that there are all sorts of highs and lows involved in the process of quilting, especially if you are developing your own design as you work, and are not following someone else's pattern. I call it the joy and the agony of quilting.

I generally start out with an idea of what colors I want to use. I think about what block, or idea, or shapes that I want to work with. I like to take a traditional block or design and distort it and change it until I am happy with the results, just like this challenge. After I do some drawings on graph paper and have a general direction to pursue, I make a swatch board of small pieces of fabric cut from the selvages and labeled as to what and where they will be used. This gives me a master plan to refer to when I get lost. Notice I said "when," not "if."

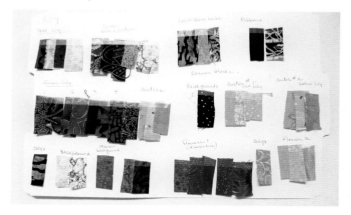

I usually print out multiple blocks on paper, so I can arrange them on the wall to see if I like where the setting is going. As I piece or appliqué, I replace the paper with "the real thing." Notice the three different versions of the cartooned lily.

The next photo shows the first partial blocks pinned up, and two border sides, which are designed from the "vase" shape at the bottom of the traditional pieced block. I moved away

from this setting because I wanted to do a more innovative version of the traditional block.

In this setting, a horizontal strippy set with the large blocks in the center are using the "border" as two of the strips.

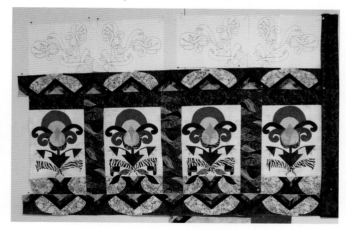

How about ribbons in the bottom space and semi-circular versions of the traditional block at the top? This would incorporate more design elements from the traditional block in the upper section.

I like trying black fabric as the background behind the Arc blocks with leaf fabric ribbons used to accent the arcs. Now the arcs finish off the tops of the folk art blocks.

So, what would happen if I made another arc block and arranged them in a semicircle over the top of the folk art block? I could do an informal vase of lilies, sort of reminiscent of the old appliqué Baltimore Album designs as the center.

I'll have to make the bouquet bigger.

Eeuuuwww! All that white makes a huge, boring lump in the middle of the quilt.

Maybe I'll frame the rectangle with the informal lilies with the border blocks. Then I'll put the arc blocks in the middle.

Omigosh! It's only two weeks until my entry has to be at the museum in Paducah and I haven't even started quilting it yet! I'll go back to the arc blocks at the top and just figure out a way to have a little space in between them so it's not so one-dimensional. I will use the petal template from the folk art lily to design the border quilting and hopefully, the rest of it will come to me as I quilt. I'm always better with a deadline!

Lynne Ott

Webster City, Iowa

Photo by Felicia Hurtt

Meet Lynne

I don't think there is a quilt that I don't like! I am inspired by other quilters and their beautiful quilts. There is so much beauty in nature to interpret and sew into a quilt. I hope to be quilting for the rest of my life.

I have been a seamstress for as long as I can remember. When I was very young I made a skirt from some old dotted swiss curtains. I've always had an interest in needlework of all kinds. When I had to make a skirt in home economics class, I got an A but it wasn't well deserved. Among other unacceptable things, it had a 9" hem. My mom was determined to teach me to sew well. I made my clothes, my children's clothes, and countless garments for other people. I even made a men's leisure suit once! I also made my daughter's wedding dress and all the other dresses in the wedding.

My interest in quilting started about 20 years ago. I soon realized that I had been using quilting techniques in my sewing all along. I purchased a Janome® embroidery machine about the time I started quilting. At that time, machine embroidery was not used in quilts. I had thoughts about how I could use it but I never did at that time.

I started going on bus trips to quilt shows and my interest grew. I first entered some small quilts in the Iowa Quilt Guild show and was quite surprised to see that they did well. I have made a few large quilts but I mostly make wallhangings and throw sizes.

My favorite and largest project was a quilted costume to be used in a local production of *Joseph and the Amazing Technicolor Dreamcoat*. It has been very well traveled, going to many quilt shows and productions of the musical in community theaters. It was at that time that I started to use machine embroidery in my quilting projects. I learned to hoop my quilt sandwich and do a lot of the quilting on my Janome 9000.

I enjoy entering my quilts in shows. I am not a highly competitive person but I appreciate the judging and constructive criticism that is given. My sense of competition is with myself. I want to improve my work and do my best. Sometimes I have a different opinion than a judge might have, but I like to try their way of doing things. It is very important to me that I do all of the work on my quilts myself. Often that means that projects don't get finished. Quilting the quilt is not my favorite part of the process.

I love traditional quilts. I love all of the patterns and the different ways you can make them look just by changing the setting. The work I do is not exactly traditional. My methods and techniques

LILIES IN THE SUNSET

53" x 53"

are a little different from the norm. I have had very little instruction and have taken very few classes. I like to ask questions of other quilters and learn from them. My quilting style falls somewhere between traditional, modern, and art quilts—maybe a combination of the three.

Inspiration & Design

I am always inspired by the beauty in nature. LILIES IN THE SUNSET is my interpretation of butterflies fluttering around beautiful lilies in a sunset.

My design for this quilt didn't begin with a plan for the completed quilt. I started with some thoughts and just kept adding ideas as I went along. I enjoy the challenge of working with ombré fabrics. There are so many interesting ways to get a different look. I also like to work with patterns, blocks, and colors that aren't my usual preferences. It stretches me to learn to do something that I wouldn't ordinarily do.

For a long time, I have had an interest in entering the New Quilts from an Old Favorite challenge. A couple of times, I even started a quilt but I didn't finish in time for the contest deadline. When I saw that the block was the Carolina Lily, I lost interest. It didn't look like my type of block. I looked for a pattern to spark my interest. I was unable to find one in my search. This was *really* getting to be a challenge! I only had the picture on the brochure to work with at that point. I looked in my Electric Quilt® BlockBase software and I found a pattern with a color photo.

There were several small setbacks in designing this quilt. I had a very limited supply of the fabrics I wanted to use, so everything had to "work" well. I had two pieces of fabric in my stash with beautiful large lilies in two colorways. I had a few ombré fabrics, one of which would coordinate well with the lily fabric.

The intense colors reminded me of a sunset. I had seen quilts with an ombré fabric cut into four large right triangles and sewn together. I wanted to use that technique so that it appeared to glow in the center. After quilting the center, I read the rules for the challenge and discovered it was about 9"–10" too small in each direction! I had nothing in my fabric collection suitable for adding as borders. After a short search, I found two striped fabrics that would work well to frame the center. The Carolina Lily was made with the unused portion of the ombré.

I like to make unusual bindings and edges. A waved edge using striped fabric added a different look to the quilt. The weaving of bias tubes evolved a little at a time. I often make machine embroidery butterflies or flowers on organza, cutting away the edge to embellish the quilt surface. That seemed like the perfect finish for my design.

Technique

The plan for my quilt started with thoughts of using an ombré fabric that faded from a berry color to pink to oranges and then to yellow. The center would be made from the same fabric into the Carolina Lily block and added to the surface after quilting. I also planned to appliqué large fabric lilies to the quilt top.

I took photos of the two fabrics and cut them apart to make a paper copy of my plan. I then found the Carolina Lily pattern on BlockBase. I printed the photo in the software and placed it on my paper quilt. My plan was to use the software templates to make the block.

I cut the ombré fabric into four large right triangles and sewed them together with the lighter color in the center. Using Hobbs Heirloom® 80/20 batting, I marked and quilted the quilt using a Gadget Girl ruler with a wave design.

Putting the Carolina Lily pattern together using the templates I printed from BlockBase didn't work well for me. So I designed my own pattern using half-square triangles and Flying Geese blocks. I drew a paper-pieced pattern for the vase and stem section. All the piecing was done on my Janome® 6600 sewing machine.

I backed the center block and made a scalloped edge around it. I stitched and turned it right-side out. The Carolina Lily block was hand appliquéd to the center of the quilt.

The bias stems were cut from a SewBatik™ dotted fabric. I sewed them and turned them using a Fasturn® tool. I cut out the fabric flowers, backed them, and stitched close to the edges by machine before turning them right-side out. I placed the stems and flowers on the quilt and they were hand appliquéd onto the quilt surface. The technique using the lilies is called *broderie perse*. If you look carefully on the right side, the stems spell my initials (LCO).

After discovering my project was too small to enter the contest, I added two striped borders. The corners are mitered. Additional quilting motifs are done on my Janome® 11000 SE Embroidery Machine using Stitchitize software.

The binding was made with a striped fabric cut on the bias to make a waved edge. Tubes of the striped fabric and the dotted batik stem fabric were hand stitched weaving in and out of the edge of the quilt.

Three butterflies were embroidered using Sulky® Solvy™ stabilizer sandwiched between two layers of organza. The edges were sealed with Dritz® Fray Check™ sealant and I trimmed the organza very close to the stitches of the butterflies. I then stitched the butterflies to the quilt surface.

At many stages during the process, I would hang the quilt on my design wall and take photos so I could analyze it to see what needed to be done next or what I needed to change. My quilts are always a work in progress. Even after finishing, I sometimes find something to add or change.

Finalist
Sue Turnquist

Tifton, Georgia

Photo by John M. Kreeger

Meet Sue

I was working in my office when I received the notice from Judy Schwender saying that she was sorry, but my entry had not been selected for the competition. I was mildly bummed (OK, so I was rolling on the floor bawling my eyes out) but, I'm a big believer in "everything happens for a reason." A few minutes later I received a second e-mail from Judy indicating that the first message was in error and that my little quilt was indeed a finalist. Whew!

As I'm heading into my "twilight" years, I'm grateful to have found my way back to quilting. My first entry to this competition was in 1999 (Kaleidoscope) when I was just a wannabe quilter. I was working full time and attempting to also quilt full time. How I long for the good old days when I had the energy to work all day and quilt all night.

During the ensuing five years, I was fortunate to have three more entries juried into this contest. As so often happens with the best-laid plans, life got in the way at that point. A midlife crisis, career change, multiple moves, and an aging parent all contributed to the gradual demise of my quilting activities. Some things occur so gradually that one doesn't realize what one has lost until it is almost irretrievable. So went my quilting, and I really didn't appreciate the void until I lost my mom in 2009. She was my rock, and as her health declined, I switched from the role of child (OK, a very old child) to the role of parent. What I couldn't see was that this

change, while entirely necessary, also robbed me of all my "me" time.

After her passing, I made the decision to return to my academic roots and relocated from New England to south Georgia (think minor culture shock). I finally had time to return to my quilting as well, but there still wasn't enough free time to satisfy the burning desire to create. I had a lot of lost time to recapture and I sure wasn't getting any younger.

I recently transitioned my day job into a part-time, 75 percent position to hopefully allow more time to devote to quilting and my beloved dogs. I had a health scare earlier this year (which fortunately turned out well) that has made me reevaluate and simplify my life. While I love my job as a veterinary pathologist, my heart remains firmly embedded in quilting, which has become more and more apparent in recent months.

I feel great sadness for those individuals who are defined by their jobs and can't imagine what they will do when they retire. I feel very blessed to know exactly what I will do—quilt full time!!!! My dream is to retire in the next few years (or months) and cultivate a second career in fiber art (or baking, if that doesn't work out). I love teaching and seeing my fiber passion spark creative fire in the next generation of quilters. I can't wait to see how the next chapter in my life's journey unfolds!

THOROUGHLY MODERN LILY

59" x 59"

Design & Inspiration

I really didn't seriously entertain the thought of constructing a Carolina Lily quilt until I surfed the Internet and saw the plethora of interpretations of this traditional block. The personal lightbulb went on as I realized this might be a fun project to tackle. As evident in my first rough sketch, my initial intention was to do a more free-form interpretation.

Then my Log Cabin obsession surfaced and the quilt segued into a somewhat symmetrical, much more controlled interpretation.

Freehand drawing is my usual *modus operandi*, but I decided to try to be a bit more controlled to maintain symmetry and balance. For the center medallion, that meant drawing half of each petal, folding the paper in half, and then using a light box to facilitate tracing the other half of the petal. One corner block was similarly drafted and then this corner served as a pattern to trace the remaining three corners. For construction, I utilized Caryl Bryer Fallert's applipiecing method.

Technique

After the center medallion and corner paper patterns were sketched, black registration marks were placed on the seam lines of the paper pattern to assist in reassembly. The paper pattern was cut apart on the seam lines. Each template of the pattern was sewn using a standard foundation paper-piecing technique. Then the components were assembled utilizing the registration marks, a light box, and Scotch® tape to join the seams in preparation for sewing.

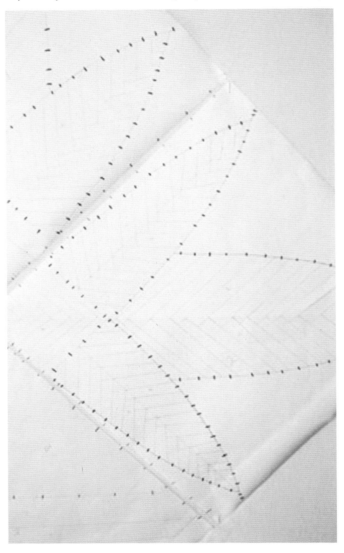

Briefly, liquid starch was painted on the seam allowance with a Q-tips® swab, and the fabric was turned to the back of the paper template using a hot iron. The light box was used to align adjacent pieced templates (using registration marks on the templates), and the tape held the aligned pieces until they were stitched. The assembled units were stitched together with invisible thread (clear for light fabrics and smoky for dark fabrics) and a tiny zigzag stitch that just caught the very edge of the folded-under top fabric. Neutral cotton thread was used in the bobbin.

Having finished the quilt with time to spare (highly unusual for me—I usually have to use overnight delivery for my entries), I was faced with the dilemma of naming the quilt. More often than not, the name comes to me before the quilt is ever born. With a finished quilt crying for a name, and no suitable name forthcoming from my dormant brain, the official entry name became *Dream Lily*. Don't know where that came from but it didn't fit, as my appraiser politely pointed out. But then she also stated that she hoped the judges would be able to recognize the Carolina Lily block.

Shortly after the meeting with the appraiser, I had a eureka moment and remembered the movie *Thoroughly Modern Millie* (with Julie Andrews—my favorite!). THOROUGHLY MODERN LILY was born!

Carolina Lily Blocks

The National Quilt Museum
Expanding the Vision, Advancing the Art

The National Quilt Museum strives to bring the work of today's quilters to new and expanding audiences worldwide. It promotes the quilting community through exhibition, education, and advocacy efforts.

Exhibits

Museum in-facility and touring exhibits are viewed by over 110,000 art enthusiasts annually. The museum is a true global destination. In an average year, visitors come to the museum from all 50 states and over 40 countries from all corners of the globe to experience the art of today's quilters. The museum's touring exhibits visit many diverse museums and galleries worldwide including the Shafer Gallery, Harlingen Arts and Heritage Museum, and Branigan Cultural Center. These exhibits feature quilts and fiber art made by some of the most respected artists working today.

Education

The museum's education programs are attended by over 4,000 youth and adults annually. Nationally renowned quilt and fiber artists conduct workshops in the museum for adult students year-round. The museum's

Velda Newman with student

youth programs fill critical art education needs and introduce thousands of kids to quilting. Several of these programs have received national media attention, including School Block Challenge sponsored by Moda. This annual contest challenges participants to incorporate three contest fabrics into a quilt block. Now in its twentieth year, this program is utilized by schools and community organizations in over 20 states as part of their art curriculum. Other popular youth programs include the annual Quilt Camp for Kids, Kidz Day in the Arts, and the Junior Quilters and Textile Artists Club.

Student in workshop

Advocacy

As part of our mission to bring quilting to new audiences, the museum works aggressively to spread the word about the extraordinary art created by today's quilt community. Last year alone, over 420 publications wrote articles about the museum's work including Reuters,

Yahoo.com, and *International Business Times*. In addition, in May 2013, the museum was featured on the internationally syndicated game show *Jeopardy*. Throughout the year museum staff members give talks and participate in panel discussions about the work of today's quilters. These efforts have had a global reach. Recently museum curator/registrar Judy Schwender spoke to a group in Beijing, China.

If you are reading these words, you are most likely one of over 21 million active quilters from the United States and around the world. The National Quilt Museum is committed to supporting your work and advancing the art of quilting so that everyone worldwide can experience and appreciate your amazing work.

For more information about The National Quilt Museum, visit our website at www. QuiltMuseum.org.

Gift shop manager Pamela Hill and volunteer Loyce Lovvo

The National Quilt Museum is a 501(c)(3) nonprofit organization funded by quilters like you.

other AQS books

This is only a small selection of the books available from the American Quilter's Society. AQS books are known worldwide for timely topics, clear writing, beautiful color photos, and accurate illustrations and patterns. The following books are available from your local bookseller, quilt shop, or public library.

#8350 . . . . $26.95

#8152 . . . . $26.95

#8669 . . . .$26.95

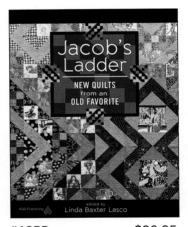

#1255 . . . . $26.95

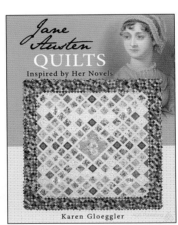

#1415 . . . .$24.95

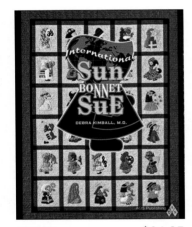

#8347 . . . .$24.95

#1423 . . . . $24.95

#1420 . . . . $24.95

#1248 . . . .$24.95

LOOK for these books nationally.
CALL or **VISIT** our website at

1-800-626-5420
www.AmericanQuilter.com